Careers in Focus

Biology

Ferguson
An imprint of ☑️®Facts On File

Careers in Focus: Biology

Copyright © 2002 by Facts On File, Inc.

Ferguson
An imprint of Facts On File, Inc.
132 West 31st Street
New York NY 10001

Library of Congress Cataloging-in-Publication Data

Careers in focus. Biology
        p. cm. — (Careers in focus)
Summary: Explores twenty-one careers in the field of biology, in terms of the nature of the work, educational or training requirements, ways to get started, advancement possibilities, salary figures, employment outlook, and sources of more information.
        ISBN 0-89434-400-5 (hardcover)
        1. Biology—Vocational guidance—Juvenile literature. [1. Biology—Vocational guidance. 2. Vocational guidance.] I. Title: Biology. II. J.G. Ferguson Publishing Company. III. Title. IV. Series.
        QH314 .C37 2001
570'.23—dc21   2001003182

Ferguson books are available at special discounts when purchased in bulk quantities for businesses, associations, institutions, or sales promotions. Please call our Special Sales Department in New York at (212) 967-8800 or (800) 322-8755.

You can find Ferguson Publishing on the World Wide Web at http://www.fergpubco.com

Managing Editor-Career Publications: Andrew Morkes
Senior Editor: Carol Yehling
Editor: Anne Paterson
Assistant Editor: Nora Walsh

Cover photo courtesy William Taufic/The Stock Market

Printed in the United States of America

MP 10 9 8 7 6 5 4 3 2

This book is printed on acid-free paper.

Table of Contents

Introduction

Biology subfields are many and varied and include microbiology, plant and animal physiology, ecology, epidemiology, cell biology, and oceanography, just to name a few. For all these areas, the elements of the job are essentially the same: building on the work of others, both past and present, through experimentation and observation.

Most research in biology uses a team approach. Team members review previous research and experiments, then set a goal for their project. They may either form a hypothesis (an educated guess) to prove or disprove a current theory, or set an open-ended objective, such as finding out what happens over time to people who smoke or drink. An experiment may prove something or not. After experimentation, the biologist analyzes the results, often publishing his or her findings in a scientific journal article. Publishing results is a key part of doing research, for only by sharing data and evaluations can the scientific community make the most of research. Scientists working under contracts with research companies do not own their discoveries; their research becomes the property of the employer. Scientists working independently can keep their discoveries as their own and have the right to patent and charge others for using their research.

Generally, those working in the biology field do one of four types of work: basic research, applied research, testing, or support. Basic research seeks knowledge for its own sake, uncovering fundamental truths and transforming the unknown into the known. Often done at universities, basic research includes all areas of biology. Applied research deals with translating basic knowledge into practical, useful products and processes for use in areas such as medicine or agriculture.

Research biologists at universities generally split their time between their research projects and teaching. High school teachers often specialize in biology and teach courses that interest them personally, such as marine biology or physiology. Because researchers need skilled help from others trained in biology, some biologists work in support roles such as laboratory technicians, who help carry out experiments. All specialists must combine a thorough knowledge of general biology with other skills and professional training.

More and more, people are doing jobs that combine their knowledge of biology with other specialized training. The "office" for many of these jobs is the outdoors and the dress is casual. Horticulturists, for example, work in greenhouses and fields, developing new crop varieties and designing landscape plans. Zookeepers may work with captive breeding programs for endangered species. Zoos, museums, and nature centers hire educators, exhibit designers, artists, and other specialists with biology backgrounds. Those with a talent for writing may work as science journalists, breaking down science so that nonexperts can understand. Other biologists work as policy analysts for the government, helping develop science-based legislation. Physicians, dentists, nurses, medical technicians, and physician's assistants must also have solid biology backgrounds.

The outlook for biologists with doctoral degrees who want to teach at a college or university is competitive for basic research positions. The increase in the number of advanced degrees, together with budget tightening for many areas of research and development, has slowed the number of grants awarded, according to the *Occupational Outlook Handbook*. Positions will continue to open up, though, as tenured faculty retire.

The outlook for jobs in private industry is better than for independent research positions, as companies respond to public concern for protecting the environment and human health. Ecologists, whose work examines environmental effects, will be needed to address such societal concerns as global warming or disappearing rain forests. Expected expansion in research related to health issues, such as AIDS, cancer, and Alzheimer's disease, should also result in growth.

Genetic researchers will be in greater demand as advances in the field of biotechnology continues. The American Institute of Biological Sciences says that plant geneticists, for example, will be needed to develop better methods of engineering crops. Researchers studying human biology will be hired in hopes of discovering ways to slow the aging process, cure genetic diseases, and reverse paralyzed nerve cells. Applications arising from new knowledge about recombinant DNA, or genetic engineering, promise to open up job opportunities, especially in the health care and pharmaceutical fields. Growing support for health-related research in general continues to provide opportunities for microbiologists, biochemists, physiologists, and other biologists.

Each article in this book discusses a particular occupation in the field of biology in detail. The articles in *Careers in Focus: Biology* appear in Ferguson's *Encyclopedia of Careers and Vocational Guidance*, but have been updated and revised with the latest information from the U.S. Department of Labor and other sources. The **Overview** section is a brief introductory description of the duties and responsibilities of someone in the career. Oftentimes, a career may have a variety of job titles. When this is the case, alternative career titles are presented in this section. The **History** section describes the history of the particular job as it relates to the overall development of its industry or field. **The Job** describes the primary and secondary duties of the job. **Requirements** discusses high school and postsecondary education and training requirements, any certification or licensing necessary, and any other personal requirements for success in the job. **Exploring** offers suggestions on how to gain some

experience in or knowledge of the particular job before making a firm educational and financial commitment. The focus is on what can be done while
still in high school (or in the early years of college) to gain a better understanding of the job. The **Employers** section gives an overview of typical
places of employment for the job. **Starting Out** discusses the best ways to
land that first job, be it through the college placement office, newspaper ads,
or personal contact. The **Advancement** section describes what kind of career
path to expect from the job and how to get there. **Earnings** lists salary ranges
and describes the typical fringe benefits. The **Work Environment** section
describes the typical surroundings and conditions of employment, whether
indoors or outdoors, noisy or quiet, social or independent, and so on. Also
discussed are typical hours worked, any seasonal fluctuations, and the stress-
es and strains of the job. The **Outlook** section summarizes the job in terms
of the general economy and industry projections. For the most part, Outlook
information is obtained from the Bureau of Labor Statistics and is supple-
mented by information taken from professional associations. Job growth
terms follow those used in the *Occupational Outlook Handbook*. Growth
described as "much faster than the average" means an increase of 36 percent
or more. Growth described as "faster than the average" means an increase of
21 to 35 percent. Growth described as "about as fast as the average" means
an increase of 10 to 20 percent. Growth described as "little change or more
slowly than the average" means an increase of 0 to 9 percent. "Decline"
means a decrease of 1 percent or more. Each article ends with **For More
Information,** which lists organizations that can provide career information on
training, education, internships, scholarships, and job placement.

Agricultural Scientists

School Subjects
Biology
Chemistry

Personal Skills
Communication/ideas
Technical/scientific

Work Environment
Indoors and outdoors
Primarily multiple locations

Minimum Education Level
Bachelor's degree

Salary Range
$24,200 to $42,340 to $79,820+

Certification or Licensing
Voluntary

Outlook
About as fast as the average

Overview

Agricultural scientists study all aspects of living organisms and the relationships of plants and animals to their environment. They conduct basic research in laboratories or in the field. They apply the results to such tasks as increasing crop yields and improving the environment. Some agricultural scientists plan and administer programs for testing foods, drugs, and other products. Others direct activities at public exhibits at such places as zoos or botanical gardens. Some agricultural scientists are professors at colleges and universities or work as consultants to business firms or the government. Others work in technical sales and service jobs for manufacturers of agricultural products. There are approximately 21,000 agricultural scientists in the United States.

History

In 1840, Justius von Liebig of Germany published *Organic Chemistry in Its Applications to Agriculture and Physiology* and launched the systematic development of the agricultural sciences. A formal system of agricultural education soon followed in both Europe and the United States. Prior to the publication of this work, agricultural developments relied on the collected experiences of farmers handed down over generations. Agricultural science has techniques in common with many other disciplines including biology, botany, genetics, nutrition, breeding, and engineering. Discoveries and improvements in these fields contributed to advances in agriculture. Some milestones include the discovery of the practice of crop rotation and the application of manure as fertilizer, which greatly increased farm yields in the 1700s. Farm mechanization was greatly advanced by the invention of the mechanical reaper in 1831 and the gasoline tractor in 1892. Chemical fertilizers were first used in the 19th century; pesticides and herbicides soon followed. In 1900, the research of a 19th-century Austrian monk, Gregor Johann Mendel, was rediscovered. He used generations of garden peas to test his theories that formed the foundation for the science of genetics.

In the 20th century, scientists and engineers were at the forefront of farm, crop, and food processing improvements. Conservationist Gifford Pinchot developed some of the first methods to prevent soil erosion in 1910, and Clarence Birdseye perfected a method of freezing food in the 1920s. Birdseye's discoveries allowed for whole new crops of produce previously too perishable for the marketplace. Engineers in the 1930s developed more powerful farm machinery, and scientists developed hybrid corn; by the 1960s, high-powered machinery, and better quality feed and pesticides were in common use. Today, advances in genetic engineering and biotechnology are leading to more efficient, economical methods of farming, and more markets for crops.

The Job

The nature of the work of the agricultural scientist can be broken down into several areas of specialization. Within each specialization there are various careers.

The following careers fall under the areas of plant and soil science:

Agronomists investigate large-scale food-crop problems, conduct experiments, and develop new methods of growing crops to ensure more efficient production, higher yields, and improved quality. They use genetic engineering to develop crops that are resistant to pests, drought, and plant diseases.

Agronomists also engage in soil science. They analyze soils to find ways to increase production and reduce soil erosion. They study the responses of various soil types to fertilizers, tillage practices, and crop rotation. Since soil science is related to environmental science, agronomists may also use their expertise to consult with farmers and agricultural companies on environmental quality and effective land use.

Botanists are concerned with plants and their environment, structure, heredity, and economic value in such fields as agronomy, horticulture, and medicine.

Horticulturists study fruit and nut orchards as well as garden plants such as vegetables and flowers. They conduct experiments to develop new and improved varieties and to increase crop quality and yields. They also work to improve plant culture methods for the landscaping and beautification of communities, parks, and homes.

Plant breeders apply genetics and biotechnology to improve plants' yield, quality, and resistance to harsh weather, disease, and insects. They might work on developing strains of wild or cultivated plants that will have a larger yield and increase profits.

Plant pathologists research plant diseases and the decay of plant products to identify symptoms, determine causes, and develop control measures. They attempt to predict outbreaks by studying how different soils, climates, and geography affect the spread and intensity of plant disease.

Another area of specialization for agricultural scientists is animal science.

Animal scientists conduct research and develop improved methods for housing, breeding, feeding, and controlling diseases of domestic farm animals. They inspect and grade livestock food products, purchase livestock, or work in sales and marketing of livestock products. They often consult agricultural businesses on such areas as upgrading animal housing, lowering mortality rates, or increasing production of animal products such as milk and eggs.

Dairy scientists study the selection, breeding, feeding, and management of dairy cattle. For example, they research how various types of food and environmental conditions affect milk production and quality. They also develop new breeding programs to improve dairy herds.

Poultry scientists study the breeding, feeding, and management of poultry to improve the quantity and quality of eggs and other poultry products.

Animal breeders specialize in improving the quality of farm animals. They may work for a state agricultural department, agricultural extension station, or university. Some of their work is done in a laboratory, but much of it is done outdoors working directly on animals. Using their knowledge of genetics, animal breeders develop systems for animals to achieve desired characteristics such as strength, fast maturation, resistance to disease, and quality of meat.

Food science is a specialty closely related to animal science, but it focuses on meeting consumer demand for food products in ways that are healthy, safe, and convenient.

Food scientists use their backgrounds in chemistry, microbiology, and other sciences to develop new or better ways of preserving, packaging, processing, storing, and delivering foods. *Food technologists* work in product development to discover new food sources and analyze food content to determine levels of vitamins, fat, sugar, and protein. Food technologists also work to enforce government regulations, inspecting food processing areas and ensuring that sanitation, safety, quality, and waste management standards are met.

Another field related to agricultural science is agricultural engineering. *Agricultural engineers* apply engineering principles to work in the food and agriculture industries. They design or develop agricultural equipment and machines, supervise production, and conduct tests on new designs and machine parts. They develop plans and specifications for agricultural buildings and for drainage and irrigation systems. They work on flood control, soil erosion, and land reclamation projects. They design food processing systems and equipment to convert farm products to consumer foods. Agricultural engineers contribute to making farming easier and more profitable through the introduction of new farm machinery and through advancements in soil and water conservation. Agricultural engineers in industry may be engaged in research or in the design, testing, or sales of equipment.

Much of the research conducted by agricultural scientists is done in laboratories and requires a familiarity with research techniques and the use of laboratory equipment and computers. Some research, however, is carried out wherever necessary. A botanist may have occasion to examine the plants that grow in the volcanic valleys of Alaska, or an animal breeder may study the behavior of animals on the plains of Africa.

Requirements

High School

Follow your high school's college preparatory program, which will include courses in English, foreign language, mathematics, and government. Also take biology, chemistry, physics, and any other science courses available. You must also become familiar with basic computer skills, including programming. It may be possible for you to perform laboratory assistant duties for your science teachers. Visiting research laboratories and attending lectures by agricultural scientists can also be helpful.

Postsecondary Training

Educational requirements for agricultural scientists are very high. A doctorate is usually mandatory for careers as college or university professors, independent researchers, or field managers. A bachelor's degree may be acceptable for some entry-level jobs, such as testing or inspecting technicians, or as technical sales or service representatives. Promotions, however, are very limited for these employees unless they earn advanced degrees.

To become an agricultural scientist, you should pursue a degree related to agricultural and biological science. As an undergraduate, you should have a firm foundation in biology, with courses in chemistry, physics, mathematics, and English. Most colleges and universities have agricultural science curriculums, although liberal arts colleges may emphasize the biological sciences. State universities usually offer agricultural science programs, too.

While pursuing an advanced degree, you'll participate in research projects and write a dissertation on your specialized area of study. You'll also do fieldwork and laboratory research along with your classroom studies.

Certification or Licensing

Agricultural scientists may choose to become a certified member of the American Registry of Certified Professionals in Agronomy, Crops, and Soils. To qualify for certification, you must earn a bachelor's degree and work five years in the field. Those with advanced degrees can qualify with less experience.

Other Requirements

As a researcher, you should be self-motivated enough to work effectively alone, yet be able to function cooperatively as part of a team. You should have an inexhaustible curiosity about the nature of living things and their environment. You must be systematic in your work habits and in your approach to investigation and experimentation and must have the persistence to continue or start over when experiments are not immediately successful.

Work performed by agricultural scientists in offices and laboratories requires intense powers of concentration and the ability to communicate one's thoughts systematically. In addition to these skills, physical stamina is necessary for those scientists who do field research in remote areas of the world.

Exploring

If you live in an agricultural community, you may be able to find part-time or summer work on a farm or ranch. A Future Farmers of America or 4-H program will introduce you to the concerns of farmers and researchers, and may involve you directly in science projects. Contact your county's extension office to learn about regional projects. You may also find part-time work in veterinarian's offices, florist shops, landscape nurseries, orchards, farms, zoos, aquariums, botanical gardens, and museums. Volunteer work is often available in zoos and animal shelters.

Employers

About 40 percent of all agricultural scientists work for federal, state, and local governments. They work within the U.S. Department of Agriculture and the Environmental Protection Agency, and for regional extension agencies and soil conservation departments. Scientists with doctorates may work on the faculty of colleges and universities. Researchers work for chemical and pharmaceutical companies, and agribusiness and consulting firms. Agricultural scientists also work in the food processing industry.

Starting Out

Agricultural scientists often are recruited prior to graduation. College or university placement offices are a source of information about jobs, and students may arrange interviews with recruiters who visit the campus.

Direct application may be made to the personnel departments of colleges and universities, private industries, or nonprofit research foundations. People interested in positions with the federal government may contact the local offices of state employment services and the U.S. Office of Personnel Management or the Federal Job Information Centers, which are located in various large cities throughout the country. Private employment agencies are another method that might be considered. Large companies sometimes conduct job fairs in major cities and will advertise them in the business sections of the local newspapers.

Advancement

Advancement in this field depends on education, experience, and job performance. Agricultural scientists with advanced degrees generally start in teaching or research and advance to administrative and management positions, such as supervisor of a research program. The number of such jobs is limited, however, and often the route to advancement is through specialization. The narrower specialties are often the most valuable.

People who enter this field with only a bachelor's degree are much more restricted. After starting in testing and inspecting jobs or as technical sales and service representatives, they may progress to advanced technicians, particularly in medical research, or become high school biology teachers. In the latter case, they must have had courses in education and meet the state requirements for teachers.

Earnings

According to the U.S. Department of Labor, the median annual salaries of agricultural scientists (from all specialty areas) was approximately $42,340 in 1998. The lowest paid 10 percent (which generally included those just starting out in the field) earned roughly $24,200, while the highest paid 10 percent made approximately $79,820 or more per year. In 1999 the U.S. Department of Labor also recorded a salary breakdown by specialty for those working for the federal government in nonsupervisory, supervisory, and managerial roles. The breakdown included the following: the average annual salary for those working in animal science was $69,400; for those working in soil science, $53,600; and for those working in horticulture, $53,800.

Unless hired for just a short-term project, agricultural scientists most likely receive health and retirement benefits in addition to their annual salary.

Work Environment

Agricultural scientists work regular hours, although researchers often choose to work longer when their experiments have reached critical points. Competition in the research field may be stiff, causing a certain amount of stress.

Agricultural scientists generally work in offices, laboratories, or classrooms where the environment is clean, healthy, and safe. Some agricultural scientists such as botanists periodically take field trips where living facilities may be primitive and strenuous physical activity may be required.

Outlook

The employment outlook for agricultural scientists looks good and is expected to grow about as fast as the average through 2008. Naturally, those with doctorates and the most experience will have the best opportunities; however, those with bachelor's and master's degrees will also find work as technicians or in farm management.

The fields of biotechnology and genetics may hold the best opportunities for agricultural scientists. New developments, such as methods of processing corn for use in medicines, will alter the marketplace. Scientists will also be actively involved in improving both the environmental impact of farming, as well as crop yields, as they focus on methods of decontaminating soil, protecting ground water, crop rotation, and other efforts of conservation. Scientists will also have the challenge of promoting these new methods to farmers.

For More Information

To learn about opportunities for scientists in the dairy industry and for information on student divisions, contact:

American Dairy Science Association
1111 North Dunlap Avenue
Savoy, IL 61874
Tel: 217-356-3182
Email: adsa@assochq.org
Web: http://www.adsa.uiuc.edu

To learn about student competitions and scholarships, contact:

American Society of Agricultural Engineering
2950 Niles Road
St. Joseph, MI 49085-9659
Tel: 616-429-0300
Email: hq@asae.org
Web: http://www.asae.org

For the free career resource guide, **Exploring Careers in Agronomy, Crops, Soils, and Environmental Sciences,** *contact:*

American Society of Agronomy
677 South Segoe Road
Madison, WI 53711
Tel: 608-273-8080
Web: http://www.agronomy.org

Aquarists

School Subjects	Biology Earth science
Personal Skills	Technical/scientific
Work Environment	Indoors and outdoors One location with some travel
Minimum Education Level	Bachelor's degree
Salary Range	$23,000 to $27,000 to $32,000
Certification or Licensing	Required
Outlook	Little change or more slowly than the average

Overview

Aquarists (pronounced, like "aquarium," with the accent on the second syllable) work for aquariums, oceanariums, and marine research institutes. They are responsible for the maintenance of aquatic exhibits. Among other duties, they feed the fish, check water quality, clean the tanks, and collect and transport new specimens.

The Job

Aquarists' work is crucial to the health of sea life in aquariums or other marine institutions. Fish require specific living conditions in their tanks; aquarists maintain the delicate water quality needed for survival in captivity. In addition to maintaining the tanks, they also keep records of the behavior and health conditions of the fish. With this information, some aquarists present special workshops for other staff members or for visitors to the aquarium.

Aquarists are not animal trainers, and do not work on marine shows. They do, however, support the staff who do. Their work is generally technical, and requires a strong science background. With increased experience and education, aquarists may, in time, become involved in research efforts at their institution or become promoted to higher professional positions such as curator.

Requirements

High School

If you want to become an aquarist, get your start in high school. Take as many science classes as you can. Biology and zoology are especially important to include in your schedule. Learn to pay attention to detail; marine science involves a good deal of careful record-keeping.

Postsecondary Training

Most aquariums, along with other institutions that hire aquarists, require that an applicant have a bachelor's degree in biological sciences, preferably with course work in such areas as parasitology, ichthyology, or other aquatic sciences. As the care of captive animals becomes a more complex discipline, it's no longer enough to apply without a four-year degree.

Certification or Licensing

Aquarists must be able to dive, in both contained water, to feed fish and maintain tanks, and in open water, on trips to collect new specimens. You'll need to have SCUBA certification, with a rescue diver classification, for this job. Potential employers will expect you to be able to pass a diving physical examination before taking you on as an aquarist.

Other Requirements

As an aquarist, you may be required to travel at different times throughout the year, to participate in research expeditions and collecting trips. On a more basic level, aquarists need to be in good physical shape, with good hearing and visual acuity. Some employers also require a certain strength level—say, the ability to regularly exert 100 pounds of force—since equipment, feed, and the animals themselves can be heavy and often unwieldy.

Exploring

In addition to formal education, many aquariums, like other types of museums, look for a strong interest in the field before hiring an applicant. Most often, they look for a history of volunteering. That means you need to look for every avenue you can find to work around fish, or other animals. Do as much as your schedule allows. Even working part-time or volunteering at a local pet store counts. Also, be sure to ask your career guidance counselor for information on marine science careers and opportunities for summer internships or college scholarships offered by larger institutes.

Employers

Aquarists most often work in zoos, public aquariums, or in research jobs with marine science institutes.

Starting Out

Full-time jobs for aquarists can be scarce, especially for those just starting in the field. Part-time or volunteer positions with zoos, aquariums, science institutes, nature centers, or even pet stores could provide valuable preliminary experience that may eventually lead to a full-time position.

Advancement

The usual career path for an aquarist progresses from intern/volunteer through part-time work to full-fledged aquarist, senior aquarist, supervisor, and finally, curator. Each step along the path requires additional experience, and often additional education. Curators generally are expected to have a Ph.D. in a relevant marine science discipline, for example. The career you build also will depend on how much hands-on work you like to do with animals. Other options are available if you are looking for a less "down and dirty" experience.

Earnings

Aquariums often are nonprofit institutions, limiting the earnings ability in this job somewhat. In general, aquarists make between $23,000 and $32,000 a year, or between about $11 and $15 per hour. Aquariums do offer fairly extensive benefits, however, including health insurance, 401-K plans, continuing education opportunities, tuition reimbursement, and reciprocal benefits with many other cultural institutions. Aquarists also can expect to travel as part of the job.

Work Environment

Aquarists may work indoors or outdoors, depending on the facility for which they work, and the exhibit to which they're assigned. Aquarists spend a lot of time in the water. Their day will be filled with a variety of tasks, some repetitive, like feeding, others unusual, such as working with rescued marine mammals, perhaps. In the beginning, aquarists work under the supervision of a senior aquarist or supervisor, and may work as part of a team.

Outlook

There is, in general, little change in the availability of positions for aquarists. While terrestrial zoos have begun to add aquarium complexes to their campuses in growing numbers, an actual boom in the construction of new aquariums is unlikely at this time. Many aquarists do advance to other positions, however, so openings do become available. The slower pace of change in this field helps underscore the need for appropriate preparation.

For More Information

For information on educational programs, summer internships, and courses, contact the following organizations:

American Zoo and Aquarium Association
8403 Colesville Road, Suite 710
Silver Spring, MD 20910-3314
Tel: 301-562-0777
Web: http://www.aza.org

Columbus Zoo Docent Association
PO Box 400
9990 Riverside Drive
Powell, OH 43065-0400
Tel: 614-645-3483
Web: http://www.colszoo.org

Marine Science Center
Northeastern University
East Point, Nahant, MA 01908
Tel: 781-581-7370
Web: http://www.dac.neu.edu/msc

Marine Science Institute
500 Discovery Parkway
Redwood CIty, CA 94063-4715
Tel: 650-364-2760
Email: info@sfbaymsi.org
Web: http://www.sfbaymsi.org

Arborists

Biology Earth science	School Subjects
Technical/scientific	Personal Skills
Primarily outdoors Primarily multiple locations	Work Environment
Bachelor's degree	Minimum Education Level
$14,560 to $30,000 to $60,000+	Salary Range
Recommended	Certification or Licensing
Faster than the average	Outlook

Overview

Arborists are professionals who practice arboriculture, which is the care of trees and shrubs, especially those found in urban areas. Arborists prune and fertilize trees and other woody plants, as well as monitor them for insects and diseases. Arborists are often consulted for various tree-related issues. The International Society of Arboriculture has a current membership of approximately 12,000 arborists, 11,000 of whom are certified.

History

Arboriculture developed as a branch of the plant science of horticulture. While related to the study of forestry, arborists view their specimens on an individual level; foresters manage trees as a group.

Trees are important to our environment. Besides releasing oxygen back to our atmosphere, trees enrich our soil with their fallen, decaying leaves, and their roots aid in the prevention of soil erosion. Trees provide shelter and a source of food for many different types of animals. People use trees as ornamentation. Trees are often planted to protect against the wind and glare of the sun, block offensive views, mark property lines, and provide privacy. Trees and shrubs often add considerably to a home's property value.

All trees need proper care and seasonal maintenance. The occupation of tree surgeon, as arborists were first known, came from the need for qualified individuals to care for trees and shrubs, as well as woody vines and ground-cover plants. Trees planted in busy city areas and in the suburbs face pollution, traffic, crowding, extreme temperatures, and other daily hazards. City trees often have a large percentage of their roots covered with concrete. Roots of larger trees sometimes interfere with plumbing pipes, sidewalks, and building foundations. Trees located along the sides of roads and highways must be maintained; branches are pruned, and fallen leaves and fruit are gathered. Proper intervention, if not prevention, of diseases is an important task of arborists.

The Job

Trees and shrubs need more than just sunlight and water. That's where arborists take over. Arborists perform many different tasks for trees and shrubs, some for the sake of maintenance and others for the tree's health and well-being.

Pruning. All trees need some amount of pruning to control their shape; sometimes limbs are trimmed if they interfere with power lines, if they cross property lines, or grow too close to houses and other buildings. Arborists may use tools such as pruning shears, or hand and power saws to do the actual cutting. If the branches are especially large or cumbersome, arborists may rope them together before the sawing begins. After cutting, the branches can be safely lowered to the ground. Ladders, aerial lifts, and cranes may be used to reach extremely tall trees. Sometimes, arborists need to cable or brace tree limbs weakened by disease or old age, or damaged by a storm.

Planting or transplanting. When cities or towns plan a new development, or wish to gentrify an existing one, they often consult with arborists to determine what types of trees to plant. Arborists can suggest trees that will thrive in a certain environment. Young plantings, or immature trees, are more cost effective and are often used, though sometimes, larger, more mature trees are transplanted to the desired location.

Diagnosis and treatment. A large part of keeping a tree healthy is the prevention of disease. There are a number of diseases that affect trees, among them anthracnose and Dutch elm disease. Insects pose a potential threat to trees, and have done considerable damage to certain species in the past, by boring into the trunk or spreading disease-causing organisms. Bacteria, fungi, viruses, and disease-causing organisms can also be fatal enemies of trees. Arborists are specially trained to identify the insect or the disease weakening the tree and apply the necessary remedy or medication. Common methods prescribed by arborists include chemical insecticides, or the use of natural insect predators to combat the problem. Arborists closely monitor insect migrations or any other situations that may be harmful to a species of tree.

When a tree is too old or badly diseased, arborists may choose to cut it down. Arborists will carefully cut the tree into pieces to prevent injury to people or damage to surrounding property.

Prevention. Trees, especially young plantings, often need extra nourishment. Arborists are trained to apply fertilizers, both natural and chemical, in a safe and environmentally friendly manner. Arborists are also hired by golf courses and parks to install lightning protection systems for lone trees or mature, valuable trees.

Requirements

High School

High school biology classes can provide you with a solid background to be a successful arborist. An interest in gardening, conservation, or the outdoors is also helpful.

Postsecondary Training

Take classes in botany, chemistry, horticulture, and plant pathology. Several colleges and universities offer arboriculture programs, and other related fields such as landscape design, nursery stock production, or grounds and turf maintenance. Entry-level positions such as assistants or climbers do not need a college degree for employment. Advanced education, however, is highly desired if you plan to make this field your career.

Certification or Licensing

The National Arborist Association (NAA) and the International Society of Arboriculture (ISA) both offer various home study courses and books on arboriculture. Most arborists are certified or licensed. Licensure ensures an arborist meets the state's regulations for working with pesticides and herbicides. Check with your local government—not all states require arborists to be licensed. Certification, given by the ISA after completion of required training and education, is considered by many as a measure of an arborist's skill and experience in the industry. Today's savvy consumers specifically look for certified arborists when it comes to caring for their trees and other precious landscaping plants. Arborists need to apply for recertification every three years, and must complete 30 units of continuing education classes and seminars.

Exploring

Interested in this field? Surfing the Internet can provide a wealth of information for you to browse. Log onto the Web sites of the NAA or the ISA for industry and career information. If you really want to test the waters, why not find summer work with an arborist? You'll earn extra spending money while at the same learning about the industry firsthand. Check with the NAA for a complete listing of certified arborists in your area.

Employers

Landscaping companies and businesses that offer a host of expert tree services are common employers of arborists. Employment opportunities are also available with municipal governments, botanical gardens, and arboretums. For example, an arborist in the Chicago area may want to seek a position with the Chicago Botanic Gardens or the Morton Arboretum; both places are known for their lush gardens and wooded trails.

Starting Out

So you've decided to become an arborist—what's the next step? Start by compiling a list of tree care firms in your area, then send your resume or fill out an application to the companies that interest you. You should also consider employment with the highway or park department of your city or county—they often hire crews to maintain their trees.

Many colleges and universities offer job placement services, or at least post employment opportunities in their office. Industry associations and trade magazines are often good sources of job openings.

Don't plan to climb to the top of an American elm your first day on the job. Expect to stay at ground level, at least for a few days. Trainees in this industry start as *helpers* or *ground workers,* who load and unload equipment from trucks, gather branches and other debris for disposal, handle ropes, and give assistance to climbers. They also operate the chipper—a machine that cuts large branches into small chips. After some time observing more experienced workers, trainees are allowed to climb smaller trees or the lower limbs of large trees. They are also taught the proper way to operate large machinery and climbing gear. Most companies provide on-the-job training that lasts from one to three months.

Advancement

Experienced arborists can advance to supervisory positions such as crew manager or department supervisor. Another option is to become a consultant in the field and work for tree care firms, city or town boards, large nurseries, or gardening groups.

Arborists with a strong entrepreneurial nature can choose to open their own business, but aspiring entrepreneurs must make sure that their business skills are up to par. Even the most talented and hard-working arborists won't stand a chance if they can't balance their accounts, or market their services properly.

Advancement to other industries related to arboriculture is another possibility. Some arborists choose to work in landscape design, forestry, or other fields of horticulture.

Earnings

According to Derick Vanice, director of education programs of the International Society of Arboriculture, entry level positions, such as grounds workers or trainees, can earn between $7 to $10 an hour; supervisors, with three or more years of experience, earn from $20 to $30 an hour; private consultants with eight to 10 years of experience, or arborists in sales positions, can earn $50,000 to $60,000 or more annually. Salaries vary greatly, depending on many factors, among them the size of the company, region, and the experience of the arborist. Arborists servicing busy urban areas tend to earn more.

Full-time employees receive a benefits package including health insurance, life insurance, paid vacation and sick time, and paid holidays. Most tree companies supply necessary uniforms, tools, equipment, and training.

Work Environment

Much of an arborist's work is physically demanding, and most of it is done outdoors. Arborists work throughout the year, though their busiest time is in the spring and summer. Tasks done at this time include fertilizing, pruning, and prevention spraying. During the winter months, arborists can expect to care for trees injured or damaged by excess snow, ice storms, or floods.

Equipment such as sharp saws, grinders, chippers, bulldozers, tractors, and other large machinery can be potentially dangerous for arborists. There is also the risk of falling from the top of a tall tree, many of which reach heights of 50 feet or more. Arborists rely on cleated shoes, security belts, and safety hoists to make their job easier, as well as safer.

Outlook

The future of arboriculture has never looked so promising. The public's increasing interest in the planning and the preservation of the environment has increased demand for qualified arborists. A healthy economy is another factor. Homeowners are willing to pay top dollar for professionally designed and maintained landscaping. According to Gallup's 1999 U.S. Homeowner Landscaping, Lawn Care, and Tree Care Survey, 24 million homeowners in the United States spent approximately 17.4 billion dollars on professional landscape and care. Research from Clemson University found that homes with professional landscaping sell for 6 to 7 percent higher than homes with lesser quality landscaping.

Increased resistance to pesticides and new species of insects pose constant threats to all trees. While travel abroad is easier and, in a sense, has made our world smaller, it has also placed our environment at risk. For example, Asian long-horn beetles were unknowingly transported to the United States via packing material. By the time the insects were discovered, the beetles had irreversibly damaged hundreds of mature trees throughout New York, Chicago, and surrounding areas. Arborists, especially those trained to diagnose and treat such cases, will be in demand to work in urban areas.

For More Information

For industry and career information, or to receive a copy of **Arborist News** *or* **Careers in Aboriculture,** *contact:*

International Society of Arboriculture
PO 3129
Champaign, IL 61826-3129
Tel: 217-355-9411
Email: isa@isa-arbor.com
Web: http://www.ag.uiuc.edu/~isa/

For industry and career information, a listing of practicing arborists, or educational programs at the university level, or home study, contact:

National Arborists Association, Inc.
3 Perimeter Road, Unit 1
Manchester, NH 03103
Tel: 603-314-5380
Web: http://www.natlarb.com

For industry information or for a copy of **City Trees,** *contact:*

Society of Municipal Arborists
PO Box 11521
St. Louis, MO 63105
Tel: 314-862-3325
Web: http://www.urban-forestry.com/

Biochemists

Overview

Biochemists explore the tiny world of the cell, study how illnesses develop, and search for ways to improve life on earth. Through studying the chemical makeup of living organisms, biochemists strive to understand the dynamics of life, from the secrets of cell-to-cell communication to the chemical changes in our brains that give us memories. Biochemists examine the chemical combinations and reactions involved in such functions as growth, metabolism, reproduction, and heredity. They also study the effect of environment on living tissue. If cancer is to be cured, the earth's pollution cleaned up, or the aging process slowed, it is likely to be biochemists and molecular biologists who are leading the way.

History

Biochemistry is a fairly new science, even though the concept of biochemistry is said to have its roots in the discovery of the fermentation process thousands of years ago. In fact, the basic steps used to make wine from grapes were the same in ancient times as they are today. However, the rather unchanging methods used for alcohol fermentation do not nearly reflect the revolutionary changes that have occurred throughout recent history in our knowledge of cell composition, growth, and function.

Robert Hooke, an English scientist, first described and named cells in 1665, when he looked at a slice of bark from an oak tree under a microscope with a magnifying power of 30x. Hooke never realized the significance of his discovery, however, because he thought the tiny boxes or "cells" he saw were unique to the bark. Anton van Leeuwenhoek, a Dutchman who lived in Hooke's time, discovered the existence of single-celled organisms by observing them in pond water and in animal blood and sperm. He used grains of sand that he had polished into magnifying glasses as powerful as 300x to see this invisible world. In 1839, nearly two centuries after Hooke's and Leeuwenhoek's discoveries, two German biologists, Matthias Schleiden and Theodor Schwann, correctly concluded that all living things consisted of cells. This theory was later expanded to include the idea that all cells come from other cells, and that the ability of cells to divide to form new cells is the basis for all reproduction, growth, and repair of many-celled organisms, like humans.

Over the past 40 years, a powerful instrument called the electron microscope has revealed the complex structure of cells. Every cell, at some state in its life, contains DNA, the genetic material that directs the cell's many activities. Biochemists have widened their scope to include the study of protein molecules and chromosomes, the building blocks of life itself. Biology and chemistry have always been allied sciences, and the exploration of cells and their molecular components, carried out by biochemists and other biological scientists, has revealed much about life. Watson and Crick's breakthrough discovery of the structure of DNA in 1953 touched off a flurry of scientific activity that led to a better and better understanding of DNA chemistry and the genetic code. These discoveries eventually made it possible to manipulate DNA, enabling genetic engineers to transplant foreign genes into microorganisms to produce such valuable products as human insulin, which occurred in 1982.

Today, the field of biochemistry crosses over into many other sciences, as biochemists have become involved in genetics, nutrition, psychology, fertility, agriculture, and more. The new biotechnology is revolutionizing the pharmaceutical industry. Much of this work is done by biochemists and molecular biologists because this technology involves understanding the complex chemistry of life.

The Job

Depending on a biochemist's education level and area of specialty, this professional can do many types of work for a variety of employers. For instance, a biochemist could have a job doing basic research for a federal government agency or for individual states with laboratories that employ skilled persons to analyze food, drug, air, water, waste, or animal tissue samples. A biochemist might work for a drug company as part of a basic research team searching for the cause of diseases or conduct applied research to develop drugs to cure disease. A biochemist might work in a biotechnology company focusing on the environment, energy, human health care, agriculture, or animal health. There, he or she might do research or quality control, or work on manufacturing/production or information systems. Another possibility is for the biochemist to specialize in an additional area, such as law, business, or journalism, and use his or her biochemistry or molecular biology background for a career that combines science with regulatory affairs, management, writing, or teaching.

Ph.D. scientists who enter the highest levels of academic life combine teaching and research. On top of teaching in university classrooms and laboratories, they also do basic research designed to increase biochemistry and molecular biology knowledge. As Ph.D. scientists, these professionals could also work for an industry or government laboratory doing basic research or research and development. The problems studied, research styles, and type of organization vary widely across different laboratories. The Ph.D. scientist may lead a research group or be part of a small team of Ph.D. researchers. Other Ph.D. scientists might opt for administrative positions. In government, for example, these scientists might lead programs concerned with the safety of new devices, food, drugs, or pesticides and other chemicals. Or they might influence which projects will get federal funding.

Generally, biochemists employed in the United States work in one of three major fields: medicine, nutrition, or agriculture. In medicine, biochemists mass-produce life-saving chemicals usually found only in minuscule amounts in the body. Some of these chemicals have been helping diabetics and heart attack victims for years. Biochemists employed in the field of medicine might work to identify chemical changes in organs or cells that signal the development of such diseases as cancer, diabetes, or schizophrenia. Or they may look for chemical explanations for why certain people develop muscular dystrophy or become obese. While studying chemical makeup and changes in these situations, biochemists may work to discover a treatment or a prevention for a disease. For instance, biochemists discovering how certain diseases such as AIDS and cancer escape detection by the immune system are also devising ways to enhance immunity to fight these diseases. Biochemists are also finding out the chemical basis of fertility and how to improve the success of in vitro fertilization to help couples have children or to preserve endangered species.

Biochemists in the pharmaceutical industry design, develop, and evaluate drugs, antibiotics, diagnostic kits, and other medical devices. They may search out ways to produce antibiotics, hormones, enzymes, or other drug components, or they may do quality control on the way in which drugs and dosages are made and determined.

In the field of nutrition, biochemists examine the effects of food on the body. For example, they might study the relationship between diet and diabetes. Biochemists doing this study could look at the nutrition content of certain foods eaten by people with diabetes and study how these foods affect the functioning of the pancreas and other organs. Biochemists in the nutrition field also look at vitamin and mineral deficiencies and how they affect the human body. They examine these deficiencies in relation to body performance, and they may study anything from how the liver is affected by a lack of vitamin B to the effects of poor nutrition on the ability to learn.

Biochemists involved in agriculture undertake studies to discover more efficient methods of crop cultivation, storage, and pest control. For example, they might create genetically engineered crops that are more resistant to frost, drought, spoilage, disease, and pests. They might focus on helping to create fruit trees that produce more fruit by studying the biochemical composition of the plant and determining how to alter or select for this desirable trait. Biochemists may study the chemical composition of insects to determine better and more efficient methods of controlling the pest population and the damage they do to crops. Or they could work on programming bacteria to clean up the environment by "eating" toxic chemicals.

About seven out of 10 biochemists are engaged in basic research, often for a university medical school or nonprofit organization, such as a foundation or research institute. The remaining 30 percent do applied research, using the discoveries of basic research to solve practical problems or develop products. For example, a biochemist working in basic research may make a discovery about how a living organism forms hormones. This discovery will lead to a scientist doing applied research, making hormones in the laboratory, and eventually to mass production. Discoveries made in DNA research have led to techniques for identifying criminals from a single strand of hair or a tiny blood stain left at the scene of a crime. The distinction between basic and applied research is one of degree, however; biochemists often engage in both types of work.

Biochemistry requires skillful use of a wide range of sophisticated analytical equipment and application of newly discovered techniques requiring special instruments or new chemical reagents. Sometimes, biochemists themselves must invent and test new instruments if existing methods and equipment do not meet their needs.

Requirements

High School

If you have an interest in biochemistry as a high school student, you should take at least one year each of biology, chemistry, physics, algebra, geometry, and trigonometry. Introductory calculus is also a good idea. Because scientists must clearly and accurately communicate their results verbally and in writing, English courses that emphasize writing skills are strongly recommended. Many colleges and universities also require several years of a foreign language, a useful skill in this day and age, as scientists frequently exchange information with researchers from other countries.

Some colleges have their own special requirements for admission, so you should do a little research and take any special courses you need for the college that interests you. Also, check the catalogs of colleges and universities to see if they offer a program in biochemistry or related sciences. Some schools award a bachelor's degree in biochemistry, and nearly all colleges and universities offer a major in biology or chemistry.

Postsecondary Training

To best prepare yourself for a career in biochemistry or molecular biology, you should start by earning a bachelor's degree in either of these two areas. Even if your college does not offer a specific program in biochemistry or molecular biology, you can get comparable training by doing one of two things: (1) working toward a bachelor's degree in chemistry and taking courses in biology, molecular genetics, and biochemistry, including a biochemistry laboratory class, or (2) earning a bachelor's degree in biology, but taking more chemistry, mathematics, and physics courses than the biology major may require, and also choosing a biochemistry course that has lab work with it.

It really doesn't matter if you earn a bachelor of science (B.S.) or a bachelor of arts (B.A.) degree; some schools even offer both. It is more important to choose your courses thoughtfully and to get advice in your freshman year from a faculty member who knows about the fields of biochemistry and molecular biology.

Many careers in biochemistry, especially those that involve teaching at a college or directing scientific research at a university, a government laboratory, or a commercial company, require at least a master's degree and prefer a doctorate or Ph.D. degree. Most students enter graduate programs with a bachelor's degree in biochemistry, or in chemistry or biology with supplementary courses. Because biochemistry and molecular biology are so broad-based, you can enter their graduate programs from such diverse fields as physics, psychology, nutrition, microbiology, or engineering. Graduate schools prefer students with laboratory or research experience.

However you get there, a graduate education program is intense. A master's degree requires about a year of course work and often a research project as well. For a Ph.D. degree, full-time course work can last up to two years, followed by one or more special test exams. But the most important part of Ph.D. training is the requirement for all students to conduct an extensive research project leading to significant new scientific findings. Most students work under a faculty member's direction. This training is vital, as it will help you develop the skills to frame scientific questions and discover ways to answer them. It will also teach you important laboratory skills useful in tackling other biochemical problems. Most students complete a Ph.D. program in four or five years.

Certification or Licensing

Biochemists who wish to work in a hospital may need certification by a national certifying board such as the American Board of Clinical Chemistry.

Other Requirements

A scientist never stops learning, even when formal education has ended. This is particularly true for biochemists and molecular biologists because constant breakthroughs and technology advances make for a constantly changing work environment. That is why most Ph.D.s go for more research experience (postdoctoral research) before they enter the workplace. As "postdocs," you would not take course work, earn a degree, or teach; you would be likely to work full-time on a high-level research project in the laboratory of an established scientist. Typically, this postdoctoral period lasts two to three years, during which time you would get a salary or be supported by a fellowship. Though not essential for many industry research jobs, postdoctoral research is generally expected of those wishing to become professors. Also, because biochemistry and medicine are such allies, some Ph.D. recipients also earn their medical degrees, or M.D.s, as a physician does. This is to get the broadest possible base for a career in medical research.

Exploring

The analytical, specialized nature of most biochemistry makes it unlikely that you will gain much exposure to it before college. Many high school chemistry and biology courses, however, allow students to work with laboratory tools and techniques that will give them a valuable background before college. In some cases, high school students can take advantage of opportunities to train as laboratory technicians by taking courses at a community college. You might also want to contact local colleges, universities, or laboratories to set up interviews with biochemists to learn as much as you can about the field. In addition, reading science and medical magazines will help you to stay current with recent breakthroughs in the biochemistry field.

Employers

Government agencies at the federal, state, and local levels employ about four out of every 10 biological scientists. At such agencies these scientists may do basic research and analyze food, drug, air, water, waste, or animal tissue samples. Biochemists also work for university medical schools or nonprofit organizations, such as a foundation or research institute, doing basic research. Drug companies employ biochemists to search for the causes of diseases or develop drugs to cure them. Biochemists work in quality control, research, manufacturing/production, or information systems at biotechnology companies that concentrate on the environment, energy, human health care, agriculture, or animal health. Universities hire biochemists to teach in combination with doing research.

Starting Out

A bachelor's degree in biochemistry or molecular biology can help you get into medical, dental, veterinary, law, or business school. It can also be a stepping stone to a career in many different but related fields: biotechnology, toxicology, biomedical engineering, clinical chemistry, plant pathology, animal science, or other fields. Biochemists fresh from a college undergraduate program can take advantage of opportunities to get valuable on-the-job experience in a biochemistry or molecular biology laboratory. The National Science Foundation and the National Institutes of Health, both federal government agencies, sponsor research programs for undergraduates. Groups who can particularly benefit from these programs include women, Hispanics, African Americans, Native Americans, Native Alaskans, and students with disabilities. Your college or university may also offer senior research projects that provide hands-on experience.

Another way to improve your chances of getting a job is to spend an additional year at a university with training programs for specialized laboratory techniques. Researchers and companies like these "certificate programs" because they teach valuable skills related to cell culture, genetic engineering, recombinant DNA technology, biotechnology, in vitro cell biology, protein engineering, or DNA sequencing and synthesis. In some universities, you can work toward a bachelor's degree and a certificate at the same time.

Biochemists with a bachelor's degree usually begin work in industry or government as research assistants doing testing and analysis. In the drug industry, for example, you might analyze the ingredients of a product to verify and maintain its quality. Biochemists with a master's degree may enter the field in management, marketing, or sales positions, whereas those with a doctorate usually go into basic or applied research. Many Ph.D. graduates work at colleges and universities where the emphasis is on teaching.

Advancement

The more education you have, the greater your reward potential. Biochemists with a graduate degree have more opportunities for advancement than those with only an undergraduate degree. It is not uncommon for students to go back to graduate school after working for a while in a job that required a lesser degree. Some graduate students become research or teaching assistants in colleges and universities, qualifying for professorships when they receive their advanced degrees. Having a doctorate allows you to design research initiatives and direct others in carrying out experiments. Experienced biochemists with doctorates can move up to high-level administrative positions and supervise entire research programs. Other highly qualified biochemists who prefer to devote themselves to research often become leaders in a particular aspect of their profession.

Earnings

According to a report by the National Association of Colleges and Employers, beginning salaries in 1999 for graduates with bachelor's degrees in biological science averaged $29,000. Those with master's degrees averaged about $34,450 in 1999, and those with doctoral degrees averaged about $45,700 that same year. The following mid-range earnings for biochemists in research and development came from a report by Abbott, Langer and Associates: $52,000 for managers, $58,064 for specialists, $83,500 for directors, and $90,479 for section heads. A report from the American Chemical Society gives the following industry earnings: $47,251 for biochemists with a bachelor's degree, $56,205 for those with a master's degree, and $79,176 for doctoral degree holders.

In the federal government, biochemists with a bachelor's degree may start out at the GS-5 level, which paid approximately $21,947 a year in 2001. A master's degree lets you start as a GS-7 or GS-9, which paid about $27,185 and $33,254, respectively, in 2001; and a doctoral degree can qualify you for the GS-11 rating, which paid approximately $40,236 in 2001. Experienced biochemists in federal positions may achieve a GS-15 rating, the highest rating for nonappointed government positions, which had a starting pay of about $79,710 in 2001. These government pay rates are also influenced by such factors as the location of the job and the experience the scientist has.

Biochemists who work for universities, the government, or industry all tend to receive good benefits packages, such as health and life insurance, pension plans, and paid vacation and sick leave. Those employed as university faculty operate on the academic calendar, which means that they can get summer and winter breaks from teaching classes.

Work Environment

Biochemists generally work in clean, quiet, and well-lighted laboratories where physical labor is minimal. They must, however, take the proper precautions in handling chemicals and organic substances that could be dangerous or cause illness. They may work with plants and animals; their tissues, cells, and products; and with yeast and bacteria.

Biochemists in industry generally work a 40-hour week, although they, like their counterparts in research, often put in many extra hours. They must be ready to spend a considerable amount of time keeping up with current literature, for example. Many biochemists occasionally travel to attend meetings or conferences. Those in research write papers for presentation at meetings or for publication in scientific journals.

Individuals interested in biochemistry must have the patience to work for long periods of time on a project without necessarily getting the desired results. Biochemistry is often a team affair, requiring an ability to work well and cooperate with others. Successful biochemists are continually learning and increasing their skills.

Outlook

Overall, employment growth for biochemists is expected to be faster than the average through 2008, and career prospects are bright for those training in any of the molecular life sciences. Competition, however, will be strong for basic research positions. Therefore, candidates with more education and the experience it brings will be more likely to find the positions they want. Employment is available in health-related fields, where the emphasis is on finding cures for such diseases as cancer, muscular dystrophy, AIDS, and mental illness. Additional jobs will be created to produce genetically engineered drugs and other products in the new and rapidly expanding field of genetic engineering. In this area, the outlook is best for biochemists with advanced degrees who can conduct genetic and cellular research. A caveat exists, however. Employment growth may slow somewhat as the number of new biotechnology firms slows and existing firms merge. Biochemists with bachelor's degrees who have difficulty entering their chosen career field may find openings as technicians or technologists or may choose to transfer their skills to other biological science fields.

It is estimated that over the next decade, 68 percent of those entering the workforce will be women and members of other minority groups. The federal government, recognizing this situation, offers a variety of special programs through the National Science Foundation and the National Institutes of Health to bring women, minorities, and persons with disabilities into the field. The field has been growing so fast that students who pursue the doctoral degree, particularly members of these groups, can expect excellent job opportunities.

For More Information

Two of the most useful sources of information about graduate programs in biochemistry are Peterson's *Annual Guides to Graduate Study, Programs in Biological, Agricultural, and Health Sciences* and the American Chemical Society's *Directory of Graduate Research.*

For additional information about careers, education, and scholarships, contact the following organizations:

American Association for Clinical Chemistry
2101 L Street, NW, Suite 202
Washington, DC 20037-1558
Tel: 800-892-1400
Web: http://www.aacc.org

American Chemical Society
1155 16th Street, NW
Washington, DC 20036
Tel: 800-227-5558
Web: http://www.acs.org

American Institute of Biological Sciences
1444 I Street, NW, Suite 200
Washington, DC 20005
Tel: 202-628-1500
Web: http://www.aibs.org

American Society for Biochemistry and Molecular Biology
Education Information
9650 Rockville Pike
Bethesda, MD 20814-3996
Tel: 301-530-7145
Web: http://www.faseb.org/asbmb

Biologists

Biology Physiology	School Subjects
Mechanical/manipulative Technical/scientific	Personal Skills
Indoors and outdoors Primarily multiple locations	Work Environment
Bachelor's degree	Minimum Education Level
$27,930 to $46,140 to $86,020+	Salary Range
Required for certain positions	Certification or Licensing
Faster than the average	Outlook

Overview

Biologists study the origin, development, anatomy, function, distribution, and other basic principles of living organisms. They are concerned with the nature of life itself—with humans, microorganisms, plants, and animals—and with the relationship of each organism to its environment. Biologists perform research in many specialties that advance the fields of medicine, agriculture, and industry.

History

The biological sciences developed slowly over the course of human history. Early humans practiced an inexact form of biology when they established agriculture. They observed the environment around them to determine what types of seeds yielded consumable food, when to plant, when to water, and when to harvest the seeds for planting in the next season. Early humans improved their way of life as a result of their primitive forays into science.

It wasn't until modern humans evolved that biology developed into an exact science. Our ancestors learned to differentiate between desirable and undesirable plants (taxonomy), to seek out and live in more habitable environments (ecology), to domesticate plants (agronomy and horticulture) and animals (animal husbandry), and to eat a suitable diet (nutrition). Eventually, plants and animals were classified; later they were studied to see how they functioned and how they related to other organisms around them. This was the beginning of zoology (animal science) and botany (plant science).

The Greek philosopher Aristotle created one of the first documented taxonomic systems for animals. He divided animals into two types: blooded (mammals, birds, amphibians, reptiles, and fishes) and bloodless (insects, crustaceans, and other lower animals). He also studied reproduction and theorized, incorrectly, how embryos developed in animals.

From the second century to the 11th century, the Arabs made important advances in biological understanding. Unlike the Europeans, they continued to study from the base of knowledge established by the Greeks. Avicenna (980-1037), a Persian philosopher and physician, wrote the *Canon of Medicine,* one of the most influential and important publications on medical knowledge in the world at its time—and for the next seven centuries.

The field of biology has expanded rapidly in the last two centuries. The French physician Louis Pasteur (1822-95) developed the field of immunology, and his studies of fermentation led to modern microbiology. Many other achievements became possible because of improvements in the microscope. Scientists could isolate much smaller structures than ever before possible. Matthias Schleiden (1804-82) and Theodor Schwann (1810-82) formulated the idea that the cell is the fundamental unit of all organisms. Gregor Mendel (1812-84) discovered the principles of heredity through the study of peas.

While the 19th century can be considered the age of cellular biology, the 20th has been dominated by studies and breakthroughs in biochemistry and molecular biology. The discovery of the atomic structure allowed the fundamental building blocks of nature to be studied. Living tissues were found to be composed of fats, sugars, and proteins. Proteins were found to be composed of amino acids. Discoveries in cell biology established the manner in which information was transmitted from one organism to its progeny. Chromosomes were recognized as the carriers of this information. In 1944 Oswald Avery and a team of scientists were able to isolate and identify DNA as the transmitter of genetic information. In 1953, James Watson and Francis Crick deciphered the complex structure of DNA and predicted that it carried the genetic code for all living matter.

Biological science is the foundation for most of the discoveries that affect people's everyday lives. Biologists break new ground to improve our health and quality of life and help us to better understand the world around us.

The Job

Biology can be divided into many specialties. The biologist, who studies a wide variety of living organisms, has interests that differ from those of the chemist, physicist, and geologist, who are concerned with nonliving matter. Biologists, or *life scientists,* may be identified by their specialties. Following is a breakdown of the many kinds of biologists and their specific fields of study:

Anatomists study animal bodies from basic cell structure to complex tissues and organs. They determine the ability of body parts to regenerate and investigate the possibility of transplanting organs and skin. Their research is applied to human medicine.

Aquatic biologists study animals and plants that live in water and how they are affected by their environmental conditions, such as the salt, acid, and oxygen content of the water and temperature, light, and other factors.

Biochemists study the chemical composition of living organisms. They attempt to understand the complex reactions involved in reproduction, growth, metabolism, and heredity.

Biophysicists apply physical principles to biological problems. They study the mechanics, heat, light, radiation, sound, electricity, and energetics of living cells and organisms and do research in the areas of vision, hearing, brain function, nerve conduction, muscle reflex, and damaged cells and tissues.

Biotechnicians, or *biological technicians,* assist the cornucopia of biological scientists in their endeavors.

Botanists study plant life. Some specialize in plant biochemistry, the structure and function of plant parts, and identification and classification, among other topics.

Cytologists, sometimes called *cell biologists,* examine the cells of plants and animals, including those cells involved in reproduction. They use microscopes and other instruments to observe the growth and division of cells and to study the influences of physical and chemical factors on both normal and malignant cells.

Ecologists examine such factors as pollutants, rainfall, altitude, temperature, and population size in order to study the distribution and abundance of organisms and their relation to their environment.

Entomologists study insects and their relationship to other life forms.

Geneticists study heredity in various forms of life. They are concerned with how biological traits such as color, size, and resistance to disease originate and are transmitted from one generation to another. They also try to develop ways to alter or produce new traits, using chemicals, heat, light, or other means.

Histopathologists investigate diseased tissue in humans and animals.

Immunologists study the manner in which the human body resists disease.

Limnologists study freshwater organisms and their environment.

Marine biologists specialize in the study of marine species and their environment. They gather specimens at different times, taking into account tidal cycles, seasons, and exposure to atmospheric elements, in order to answer questions concerning the overall health of sea organisms and their environment.

Microbiologists study bacteria, viruses, molds, algae, yeasts, and other organisms of microscopic or submicroscopic size. Some microorganisms are useful to humans; they are studied and used in the production of food, such as cheese, bread, and tofu. Other microorganisms have been used to preserve food and tenderize meat. Some microbiologists work with microorganisms that cause disease. They work to diagnose, treat, and prevent disease. Microbiologists have helped prevent typhoid fever, influenza, measles, polio, whooping cough, and smallpox. Today, they work on cures for AIDS, cancer, cystic fibrosis, and Alzheimer's disease, among others.

Molecular biologists apply their research on animal and bacterial systems toward the goal of improving and better understanding human health.

Mycologists study edible, poisonous, and parasitic fungi, such as mushrooms, molds, yeasts, and mildews, to determine which are useful to medicine, agriculture, and industry. Their research has resulted in benefits such as the development of antibiotics, the propagation of mushrooms, and methods of retarding fabric deterioration.

Nematologists study nematodes (roundworms), which are parasitic in animals and plants. Nematodes transmit diseases, attack insects, or attack other nematodes that exist in soil or water. Nematologists investigate and develop methods of controlling these organisms.

Parasitologists study animal parasites and their effects on humans and other animals.

Pharmacologists may be employed as researchers by pharmaceutical companies. They often spend most of their time working in the laboratory, where they study the effects of various drugs and medical compounds on mice or rabbits. Working within controlled environments, pharmacologists precisely note the types, quantities, and timing of medicines administered as a part of their experiments. Periodically, they make blood smears or perform autopsies to study different reactions. They usually work with a team of researchers, headed by one with a doctorate and consisting of several biologists with master's and bachelor's degrees and some laboratory technicians.

Physiologists are biologists who specialize in studying all the life stages of plants or animals. Some specialize in a particular body system or a particular function, such as respiration.

Wildlife biologists study the habitats and the conditions necessary for the survival of birds and other wildlife. Their goal is to find ways to ensure the continuation of healthy wildlife populations, while lessening the impact and growth of civilization around them.

Zoologists study all types of animals to learn their origin, interrelationships, classifications, life histories, habits, diseases, relation to the environment, growth, genetics, and distribution. Zoologists are usually identified by the animals they study: *ichthyologists* (fish), *mammalogists* (mammals), *ornithologists* (birds), and *herpetologists* (reptiles and amphibians).

Biologists may also work for government agencies concerned with public health. *Toxicologists,* for example, study the effects of toxic substances on humans, animals, and plants. The data they gather are used in consumer protection and industrial safety programs to reduce the hazards of accidental exposure or ingestion. Public-health microbiologists conduct experiments on water, foods, and the general environment of a community to detect the presence of harmful bacteria so pollution and contagious diseases can be controlled or eliminated.

Requirements

High School

High school students interested in a career in biology should take English, biology, physics, chemistry, Latin, geometry, and algebra.

Postsecondary Training

Prospective biologists should also obtain a broad undergraduate college training. In addition to courses in all phases of biology, useful related courses include organic and inorganic chemistry, physics, and mathematics. Modern languages, English, biometrics (the use of mathematics in biological measurements), and statistics are also useful. Courses in computers will be extremely beneficial. Students should take advantage of courses that require laboratory, field, or collecting work.

Nearly all institutions offer undergraduate training in one or more of the biological sciences. These vary from liberal arts schools that offer basic majors in botany and zoology to large universities that permit specialization in areas such as entomology, bacteriology, and physiology at the undergraduate level.

The best way to become a biologist is to earn a bachelor's degree in biology or one of its specialized fields, such as anatomy, bacteriology, botany, ecology, or microbiology. For the highest professional status, a doctorate is required. This is particularly true of top research positions and most higher-level college teaching openings. Many colleges and universities offer courses leading to a master's degree and a doctorate. A study made by the National Science Foundation showed that among a group of biologists listed with the National Scientific Manpower Register, 10 percent held a bachelor's degree, 33 percent held a master's or professional medical degree, and the remaining 57 percent had earned a doctorate.

Candidates for a doctorate specialize in one of the subdivisions of biology. A number of sources of financial assistance are available to finance graduate work. Most major universities have a highly developed fellowship (scholarship) or assistantship (part-time teaching or research) program.

Organizations, such as the U.S. Public Health Service and the National Science Foundation, make awards to support graduate students. In a recent year, for example, the Public Health Service made 8,000 fellowship and training grants. In addition, major universities often hold research contracts or have their own projects that provide part-time and summer employment for undergraduate and graduate students.

Certification or Licensing

A state license may be required for biologists who are employed as technicians in general service health organizations, such as hospitals or clinics. To qualify for this license, proof of suitable educational background is necessary.

Other Requirements

Biologists must be systematic in their approach to solving the problems that they face. They should have probing, inquisitive minds and an aptitude for biology, chemistry, and mathematics. Patience and imagination are also required since they may spend much time in observation and analysis. Biologists must also have good communication skills in order to effectively gather and exchange data and solve problems that arise in their work.

Exploring

Students can measure their aptitude and interest in the work of the biologist by taking courses in the field. Laboratory assignments, for example, provide information on techniques used by the working biologist. Many schools hire students as laboratory assistants to work directly under a teacher and help administer the laboratory sections of courses.

School assemblies, field trips to federal and private laboratories and research centers, and career conferences provide additional insight into career opportunities. Advanced students often are able to attend professional meetings and seminars.

Part-time and summer positions in biology or related areas are particularly helpful. Students with some college courses in biology may find summer positions as laboratory assistants. Graduate students may find work on research projects conducted by their institutions. Beginning college and advanced high school students may find employment as laboratory aides or hospital orderlies or attendants. Despite the menial nature of these positions, they afford a useful insight into careers in biology. High school students often have the opportunity to join volunteer service groups at local hospitals. Student science training programs allow qualified high school students to spend a summer doing research under the supervision of a scientist.

Employers

Over 400 firms employ biotechnologists in the United States, mainly in the West, Midwest, and East. Many companies, such as pharmaceutical firms, operate throughout the nation. Herpetologists will find employment in zoos or museums and in research laboratories assisting with projects. Those with broader interests may choose to work in local, state, or national parks as park naturalists or for certain companies as environmental specialists. Marine biologists might find employment with the U.S. Department of Interior, the U.S. Fish and Wildlife Service, and the National Oceanic and Atmospheric Administration. They may also find employment in nongovernmental agencies, such as the Scripps Institution of Oceanography in California and the Marine Biological Laboratory in Massachusetts. Microbiologists can find employment with the U.S. Department of Health and Human Services, the Environmental Protection Agency, and the Department of Agriculture, among others. They may also work for pharmaceutical, food, agricultural, geological, environmental, and pollution control companies. Wildlife biologists can find employment for the U.S. Public Health Service, the U.S. Fish and Wildlife Service, and the Forest Service, among many others.

Starting Out

Biologists who are interested in becoming teachers should consult their college placement offices. Public and private high schools and an increasing number of colleges hire teachers through the colleges at which they studied. Private employment agencies also place a significant number of teachers. Some teaching positions are filled through direct application.

Biologists interested in private industry and nonprofit organizations may also apply directly for employment. Major organizations that employ biologists often interview college seniors on campus. Private and public employment offices frequently have listings from these employers. Experienced biologists often change positions as a result of contacts made at professional seminars and national conventions.

Special application procedures are required for positions with government agencies. Civil service applications for federal, state, and municipal positions may be obtained by writing to the agency involved and from high school and college guidance and placement bureaus, public employment agencies, and post offices.

Advancement

In a field as broad as biology, numerous opportunities for advancement exist. To a great extent, however, advancement depends on the individual's level of education. A doctorate is generally required for college teaching, independent research, and top-level administrative and management jobs. A master's degree is sufficient for some jobs in applied research, and a bachelor's degree may qualify for some entry-level jobs.

With the right qualifications, the biologist may advance to the position of project chief and direct a team of other biologists. Many use their knowledge and experience as background for administrative and management positions. Often, as they develop professional expertise, biologists move from strictly technical assignments into positions in which they interpret biological knowledge.

The usual path of advancement in biology, as in other sciences, comes from specialization and the development of the status of an expert in a given field. Biologists may work with professionals in other major fields to explore problems that require an interdisciplinary approach, such as biochemistry, biophysics, biostatistics (or biometrics). Biochemistry, for example, uses the methods of chemistry to study the composition of biological materials and the molecular mechanisms of biological processes.

Earnings

Salaries for all biological scientists range from $27,930 to over $86,020, with a median salary of $46,140, as reported by the U.S. Department of Labor. In 1999, biologists with bachelor's degrees who worked for the federal government earned average salaries of $56,000 a year; ecologists averaged $57,100; microbiologists averaged $62,600; and geneticists, $68,200.

According to the National Association of Colleges and Employers, biologists with bachelor's degrees who worked in private industry averaged beginning salaries of $29,000 a year in 1999. Those with master's degrees earned $34,450, and doctoral degree recipients earned about $45,700. Most earned an average of $28,400 to $50,900 a year. In general, the highest salaries were earned by biologists in business and industry, followed by those self-employed, working for nonprofit organizations, in military service, and working for the U.S. Public Health Service or other positions in the federal government. The lowest salaries were earned by teachers and by those working for various state and local governments.

Some examples of salaries for specific careers follow. Biotechnologists with a master's degree earn about $37,000 a year, while those with a doctorate can earn more than $80,000. Microbiologists employed at educational institutes earn between $16,000 and $30,000 with a bachelor's degree, between $20,000 and $60,000 with a master's degree, and between $30,000 and $100,000 with a Ph.D. Those in industry make very similar amounts on the whole as those in educational institutions. Microbiologists employed by the government and in the private sector with a bachelor's degree earn $17,000 to $33,000 a year; those with a master's earn from $20,000 to $45,000 a year, and those with a Ph.D. earn from $30,000 to $90,000. Biotechnicians earn between $13,000 and $50,000 per year, with an average median salary of approximately $26,000.

Biologists are usually eligible for health and dental insurance, paid vacations and sick days, and retirement plans. Some employers may offer reimbursement for continuing education, seminars, and travel.

Work Environment

The biologist's work environment varies greatly depending upon the position and type of employer. One biologist may work outdoors or travel much of the time. Another wears a white smock and spends years working in a laboratory. Some work with toxic substances and disease cultures; strict safety measures must be observed.

Biologists frequently work under pressure. For example, those employed by pharmaceutical houses work in an atmosphere of keen competition for sales that encourages the development of new drug products, and, as they are identified, the rapid testing and early marketing of these products. The work is very exacting, however, and pharmaceutical biologists must exercise great care to ensure that adequate testing of products has been properly conducted.

Some biologists, including botanists, ecologists, and zoologists, may undertake strenuous, sometimes dangerous, fieldwork in primitive conditions. Marine biologists work in the field, on research ships or in laboratories, in tropical seas and ocean areas with considerably cooler climates. They will be required to perform some strenuous work, such as carrying a net, digging, chipping, or hauling equipment or specimens. Marine biologists who work under water must be able to avoid hazards, such as razor-sharp coral reefs and other underwater dangers. Wildlife biologists work in all types of weather and in all types of terrain and ecosystems. They may work alone or with a group in inhospitable surroundings in order to gather information.

Outlook

The U.S. Department of Labor predicts a faster-than-average increase in employment of biologists through 2008, although competition will be stiff for high-paying jobs, and government jobs will be less plentiful.

Advances in genetic research leading to new drugs, improved crops, and medical discoveries should open up some opportunities. Expanded research relating to cancer, AIDS, and the Human Genome project should also offer additional jobs to highly qualified biologists. It is important to note that since many of these projects are funded by the federal government, their growth is not assured. A recession or shift in political power could cause the loss of funding for grants and the decline of research and development endeavors. Private industry will need more biologists to keep up with the advances in biotechnology. Efforts to preserve and clean up the environment will create more job opportunities for qualified biologists.

Biologists with advanced degrees will be best qualified for the most lucrative and challenging jobs, although this varies by specialty, with genetic, cellular, and biochemical research showing the most promise. Scientists with only a bachelor's degree may find openings as science or engineering technicians or as health technologists and technicians. Many colleges and universities are cutting back on their faculties, but high schools and two-year colleges may have teaching positions available. High school biology teachers are not considered to be biologists, however.

Because biologists are usually employed on long-term research projects or in agriculture, areas that are not greatly affected by economic fluctuations, they rarely lose their jobs during recessions. In 1998, over 112,000 biologists and medical scientists were employed in the United States. Many worked at the college and university level. Others worked in research and development laboratories for private industry, mainly in pharmaceutical, chemical, and food companies. About 40 percent were employed by the federal government and by state and local governments. Some held nonteaching positions at colleges or universities; others worked for nonprofit research organizations or hospitals or were self-employed.

For More Information

For information on careers in biology, contact:

American Institute of Biological Sciences
1444 I Street, NW, Suite 200
Washington, DC 20005
Tel: 202-628-1500
Web: http://www.aibs.org

For a career brochure, career-related articles, and a list of institutions that award academic degrees with a major in physiology, contact:

American Physiological Society
9650 Rockville Pike
Bethesda, MD 20814-3991
Tel: 301-530-7164
Web: http://www.faseb.org/aps

For information on careers, educational resources, and fellowships, contact:

American Society for Microbiology
1752 N Street, NW
Washington, DC 20036
Tel: 202-737-3600
Web: http://www.asmusa.org

For information on specific careers, contact the FDA's job hotline:

Food and Drug Administration (FDA)
5600 Fishers Lane
Rockville, MD 20857
Tel: 888-463-6332
Web: http://www.fda.gov/

For career information, including articles and books, contact:

Biotechnology Industry Organization
1625 K Street, NW, Suite 1100
Washington, DC 20006
Tel: 202-857-0244
Web: http://www.bio.org

For information on careers in the marine sciences, contact:

National Aquarium in Baltimore
501 East Pratt Street, Pier 3
Baltimore, MD 21202-3194
Tel: 410-576-3800
Web: http://www.aqua.org/

For information on specific careers in biology, contact:

National Institutes of Health
National Center for Research Resources
Tel: 301-496-4000
Email: NIHInfo@OD.NIH.GOV
Web: http://www.nih.gov/

Biomedical Engineers

	School Subjects
Biology Chemistry	

	Personal Skills
Helping/teaching Technical/scientific	

	Work Environment
Primarily indoors Primarily one location	

	Minimum Education Level
Bachelor's degree	

	Salary Range
$25,000 to $45,000 to $65,000	

	Certification or Licensing
Voluntary	

	Outlook
Faster than the average	

Overview

Biomedical engineers are highly trained scientists who use engineering and life science principles to research biological aspects of animal and human life. They develop new theories, and they modify, test, and prove existing theories on life systems. They design health care instruments and devices or apply engineering principles to the study of human systems.

History

Biomedical engineering is one of many new professions created by advancements in technology. It is an interdisciplinary field that brings together two respected professions: biology and engineering.

Biology, of course, is the study of life, and engineering, in broad terms, studies sources of energy in nature and the properties of matter in a way that is useful to humans, particularly in machines, products, and structures. A combination of the two fields, biomedical engineering developed primarily after 1945, as new technology allowed for the application of engineering principles to biology. The artificial heart is just one in a long list of the products of biomedical engineering. Other products include artificial organs, prosthetics, the use of lasers in surgery, cryosurgery, and ultrasonics, and the use of computers and thermography in diagnosis.

The Job

Using engineering principles to solve medical and health-related problems, the biomedical engineer works closely with life scientists, members of the medical profession, and chemists. Most of the work revolves around the laboratory. There are three interrelated work areas: research, design, and teaching.

Biomedical research is multifaceted and broad in scope. It calls upon engineers to apply their knowledge of mechanical, chemical, and electrical engineering as well as anatomy and physiology in the study of living systems. Using computers, biomedical engineers use their knowledge of graphic and related technologies to develop mathematical models that simulate physiological systems.

In biomedical engineering design, medical instruments and devices are developed. Engineers work on artificial organs, ultrasonic imagery devices, cardiac pacemakers, and surgical lasers, for example. They design and build systems that will update hospital, laboratory, and clinical procedures. They also train health care personnel in the proper use of this new equipment.

The teaching aspect of biomedical engineering is on the university level. Teachers conduct classes, advise students, serve on academic committees, and supervise or conduct research.

Within biomedical engineering, an individual may concentrate on a particular specialty area. Some of the well-established specialties are bioinstrumentation, biomechanics, biomaterials, systems physiology, clinical engineering, and rehabilitation engineering. These specialty areas frequently depend on one another.

Biomechanics is mechanics applied to biological or medical problems. Examples include the artificial heart, the artificial kidney, and the artificial hip.

Systems physiology uses engineering strategies, techniques, and tools to gain a comprehensive and integrated understanding of living organisms ranging from bacteria to humans. Biomedical engineers in this specialty examine such things as the biochemistry of metabolism and the control of limb movements.

Rehabilitation engineering is a new and growing specialty area of biomedical engineering. Its goal is to expand the capabilities and improve the quality of life for individuals with physical impairments. Rehabilitation engineers often work directly with the disabled person and modify equipment for individual use.

Requirements

High School

You can best prepare for a career as a biomedical engineer by taking courses in biology, chemistry, physics, mathematics, drafting, and computers. Communication and problem-solving skills are necessary, so classes in English, writing, and logic are important. Participation in science clubs and competing in science fairs will give you the opportunity to design and invent systems and products.

Postsecondary Training

Most biomedical engineers have an undergraduate degree in biomedical engineering or a related field and a Ph.D. in some facet of biomedical engineering. Undergraduate study is roughly divided into halves. The first two years are devoted to theoretical subjects, such as abstract physics and differential equations in addition to the core curriculum most undergraduates take. The third and fourth years include more applied science. Worldwide, there are over 80 colleges and universities that offer programs in biomedical engineering.

During graduate programs, students work on research or product development projects headed by faculty.

Certification or Licensing

Engineers whose work may affect the life, health, or safety of the public must be registered according to regulations in all 50 states and the District of Columbia. Applicants for registration must have received a degree from an American Board for Engineering and Technology-accredited engineering program and have four years of experience. They must also pass a written examination administered by the state they wish to work in.

Other Requirements

You should have a strong commitment to learning if you plan on becoming a biomedical engineer. You should be scientifically inclined and be able to apply that knowledge in problem solving. Becoming a biomedical engineer requires long years of schooling because a biomedical engineer needs to be an expert in the fields of engineering and biology. Also, biomedical engineers have to be familiar with chemical, material, and electrical engineering as well as physiology and computers.

Exploring

Undergraduate courses offer a great deal of exposure to the field. Working in a hospital where biomedical engineers are employed can also provide you with insight into the field, as can interviews with practicing or retired biomedical engineers.

Employers

There are more than 4,000 biomedical engineers in the United States. Biomedical engineers are frequently employed in hospitals and medical institutions, and in research and educational facilities. Employment opportunities also exist in industry and government regulatory agencies.

Starting Out

A variety of routes may be taken to gain employment as a biomedical engineer. Recent graduates may use college placement services, or they may apply directly to employers, often to personnel offices in hospitals and industry. A job may be secured by answering an advertisement in the employment section of a newspaper. Information on job openings is also available at the local office of the U.S. Employment Service.

Advancement

Advancement opportunities are tied directly to educational and research background. In a nonteaching capacity, a biomedical engineer with an advanced degree can rise to a supervisory position. In teaching, a doctorate is usually necessary to become a full professor. By demonstrating excellence in research, teaching, and departmental committee involvement, one can move from instructor to assistant professor and then to full professor, department chair, or even dean.

Qualifying for and receiving research grant funding can also be a means of advancing one's career in both the nonteaching and teaching sectors.

Earnings

How much a biomedical engineer earns is dependent upon education and experience. Salaries for biomedical engineers range from $25,000 to $65,000. Those with advanced degrees hold the higher-paying positions, while those with minimum education (bachelor's degree) hold the lower-paying positions.

According to the National Association of Colleges and Employers, average beginning salary offers in private industry in 2000 were $44,863 a year for those with a bachelor's degree in bioengineering and biomedical engineering, and about $50,433 for those with a master's degree.

Salaries for college and university teachers ranged from $33,400 for instructors to $72,700 for professors, according to a 1998-99 survey by the American Association of University Professors. University professors can supplement their income significantly by writing and consulting.

Work Environment

Biomedical engineers who teach in a university will have much student contact in the classroom, the laboratory, and the office. They also will be expected to serve on relevant committees while continuing their teaching, research, and writing responsibilities. As competition for teaching positions increases, the requirement that professors publish papers will increase. Professors usually are responsible for obtaining government or private research grants to support their work.

Outlook

It is expected that there will be a greater need for skilled biomedical engineers in the future. Prospects look particularly good in the health care industry, which will continue to grow rapidly, primarily because people are living longer. The U.S. Department of Labor predicts that engineering jobs in health care will grow by 33.4 percent from 1998 to 2008. New jobs will become available in biomedical research in prosthetics, artificial internal organs, computer applications, and instrumentation and other medical systems. In addition, a demand will exist for teachers to train the biomedical engineers needed to fill these positions.

For More Information

For more information on careers in biomedical engineering, contact:

American Society for Engineering Education
1818 N Street, NW
Washington, DC 20036
Tel: 202-331-3500
Web: http://www.asee.org

For information on careers, student chapters, and to obtain the brochure, Planning a Career in Biomedical Engineering, *contact:*

Biomedical Engineering Society
8401 Corporate Drive, Suite 110
Landover, MD 20785-2224
Tel: 301-459-1999
Web: http://mecca.org/BME/BMES/society

For information on high school programs that provide opportunities to learn about engineering technology, contact JETS:

Junior Engineering Technical Society, Inc. (JETS)
1420 King Street, Suite 405
Alexandria, VA 22314-2794
Tel: 703-548-5387
Email: jets@nae.edu
Web: http://www.jets.org

For Canadian career information, contact:

Canadian Medical and Biological Engineering Society
Society Secretariat
PO Box 51023
Orleans ON K1E 3W4 Canada
Tel: 613-837-8649
Email: secretariat@cmbes.ca
Web: http://www.cmbes.ca/

Visit the following Web site for more information on educational programs, job listings, grants, and links to other biomedical engineering sites:

The Biomedical Engineering Network
Web: http://www.bmenet.org

Biotechnology Patent Lawyers

School Subjects
| Biology
| Chemistry
| English

Personal Skills
| Communication/ideas
| Technical/scientific

Work Environment
| Primarily indoors
| Primarily multiple locations

Minimum Education Level
| Doctorate

Salary Range
| $60,000 to $125,000
| to $250,000+

Certification or Licensing
| Required by all states

Outlook
| About as fast as the average

Overview

Biotechnology patent lawyers are lawyers who specialize in helping biotechnology researchers, scientists, and research corporations with all legal aspects of their biotechnology patents. They assist clients in applying for patents and enforcing those patents. Although some of their duties may be similar to those of intellectual property lawyers, these lawyers focus on work involving the biotechnology field.

History

Biotechnology patent law is a blending of two fields: science and law. The field of science dates back thousands of years. Ancient Egyptians, for example, organized knowledge about matter into systems, which was the beginning of chemistry. In the 4th century BC, the field of biology advanced with the work of Greek philosopher Aristotle, who created taxonomic (classification) systems for animals. The 11th-century Persian philosopher and physician Avicenna wrote the *Canon of Medicine,* a compendium of medical knowledge. In the 19th century, Louis Pasteur, Matthias Schleiden, and Theodor Schwann contributed to the growth of the field of microbiology; Gregor Mendel discovered the principles of genetics through his studies of peas. The modern history of genetics can be traced back to the early 1950s when James Watson and Francis Crick discovered the double helix structure of DNA, the genetic material that makes up the most basic component of living organisms. After that came the discovery of recombinant DNA techniques and finally the ability to genetically engineer cells and clone (make copies of) desired genes. These scientific advancements have resulted in such developments as nontoxic pesticides, longer lasting vegetables, advanced blood tests, and even Dolly, the cloned Scottish sheep.

The history of law also dates back thousands of years, although the area of patent law has been a relatively recent development. Dating back to the 1700s, people sought help from lawyers to protect their ideas and inventions from theft. Unfortunately, both lawyers and their clients were often frustrated in their attempts to gain support for patents and copyrights in court. By the 20th century, however, Congress and courts had begun to see innovative ideas and products as valuable to U.S. status in the global market. Today, scientists, researchers, and research companies involved with biotechnology rely on patent law to ensure that their discoveries and advancements are protected as their property. Biotechnology patent lawyers are the unique bridge between the scientific and legal worlds, making sure their clients receive the acknowledgements for and profits from their scientific work.

The Job

The biotechnology patent lawyer's job actually begins only after researchers or scientists have done extensive work in their field. For example, researchers or scientists may draw on advances in molecular and cellular biology, genetics, and knowledge of the human immune system, to change and combine DNA in an effort to come up with a new vaccine. When they have developed this vaccine, they are ready to seek a patent for their invention from the Patent and Trademark Office. At this point, biotechnology patent lawyers join the process to help these researchers and research corporations with all legal aspects of their biotechnology patents. A patent gives the patent holder the right to exclude others from making, using, or selling an invention for a specific period of time.

Biotechnology patent lawyers have extensive scientific and legal knowledge. Like any other lawyer, they must be able to give clients legal advice and represent them in court when necessary. In addition, their scientific knowledge helps them prepare patent specifications for their clients' work.

For most biotechnology patent attorneys, the job falls into three major categories. First, they take their clients' patent claims before the Patent and Trademark Office and attempt to obtain patents for them. Second, they negotiate various kinds of business transactions that involve patents. For example, they might assist a client in licensing the rights to use or sell a certain patented technology. Third, biotechnology lawyers assist clients in the enforcement of patents, which might involve suing another party for patent infringement or defending a client from an infringement lawsuit. While some patent attorneys may find that most of their cases fall into one or the other of these categories, most patent attorneys take on cases in all three of these areas.

According to Lawrence Foster, a biotechnology patent attorney who practices on the East Coast, the best part of biotech practice is the chance to learn about the latest scientific discoveries and developments. "You can open a newspaper and see the first article will feature something you've known about for months," he remarks. "It's exciting to know that you're learning about these discoveries as they happen, long before most people have any idea." Although lawyers must keep these often thrilling developments quiet to protect their clients' confidentiality, they still have the satisfaction of knowing that they're party to the latest inventions in genetic and even cloning technology.

Requirements

High School

To prepare for this field, take college preparatory classes in high school that include both the sciences, such as biology and chemistry, and government or law. In addition, take mathematics and economics classes, which will give you practice working with numbers and theories. Take history or social studies courses, which will provide you with an understanding of the development of societies. Since much of your professional time will be spent researching documents, writing patent specifications, and presenting arguments, be sure to take English classes. These classes will help you develop your writing, speaking, and research skills. Finally, since many colleges have a foreign language requirement and biotechnology work takes place around the world, consider adding a language to your class schedule.

Postsecondary Training

Because this is a specialized field, you will need several years of postsecondary training that include undergraduate and graduate level work. Like any lawyer, you will need to get a college degree before attending law school. A liberal arts background is the most common to have. In addition to such courses as English, government, and economics, you will also want to load up on science courses and should consider majoring in one of the sciences. In fact, biotechnology patent lawyers in the greatest demand typically have Ph.D.s in a science field, such as genetic engineering, as well as their law degree. After college, a Ph.D. in one of the sciences may take between four and five years to complete. Law school typically lasts three years for full-time students. As part of their entrance requirements, most law schools require potential students to take the Law School Admission Test (LSAT), which measures critical thinking and reasoning abilities. In law school you will take such classes as legal writing and research, contracts, constitutional law, and property. You should also take courses in intellectual property law, which are necessary for any type of patent lawyer. You will graduate from law school with a juris doctor (J.D.) degree or a bachelor of laws (LL.B.) degree.

Certification or Licensing

To practice any type of law, you must pass the bar exam of the state where you intend to practice. To qualify for the bar exam in most states, you must usually have a college degree as well as a law degree from a law school accredited by the American Bar Association. Many find these requirements are tough enough, but would-be patent lawyers have a much longer and harder road to travel before they can practice. First, all patent attorneys must pass another bar exam specific to patent law and given by the Patent and Trademark Office. Patent attorneys must then also prove that they have at least an undergraduate degree in one of the scientific fields that has been approved by the Patent and Trademark Office.

Other Requirements

While scientific aptitude and knowledge are clearly important for achieving success in this field, verbal skills tend to be at least as important as the more analytic, scientific ones. "When you're dealing with someone who has invented a specific technology," Lawrence Foster remarks, "you're dealing with probably one of the most knowledgeable people in this particular scientific area in the whole world." While just communicating with the inventor may take all your skill and scientific background, the even greater challenge often comes when you have to communicate that specialized and technical knowledge to a judge who may have no scientific training. "As a biotech patent attorney, your job often requires translating from the most specialized to the most general kinds of language," Foster sums up. "That takes just as much verbal skill as it does scientific knowledge."

Exploring

Since biotechnology patent law combines the areas of science and law, there are a number of ways you can explore this field. To investigate the law aspect of this career, try to get a part-time job or internship with a law office in your area. You will probably be doing tasks such as filing papers, photocopying, and answering phones, but this experience will give you an idea of what working in a law office is like. If you can't find such a job, try locating a lawyer in your area with whom you could do an informational interview. Even if the lawyer is not a biotechnology patent lawyer, he or she may be able to give you some insights into the practice of law and the experience of law school.

To explore the science aspects of this career, consider joining a science or engineering club at your school. Ask your science teacher about any contacts he or she might have with scientists at the university level. You may be able to set up an informational interview with a scientist working on or having completed a Ph.D. Find out what this person likes about the field and get any advice he or she may offer to a young scientist.

Employers

Many biotechnology patent attorneys work for law firms that focus on biotechnology patent law or intellectual property law, although some practice at firms that offer a wider range of legal specialties. Other lawyers practice at larger biotechnology corporations that hire their own in-house counsels, or at the Patent and Trademark Office itself. For all biotechnology patent lawyers, however, the work environment tends to be formal and often intense, since the amount of money at issue in biotechnology patent suits is usually substantial. Biotechnology patent law tends to be most active in areas where the industry itself is strong; currently, these areas include Boston, San Francisco, San Diego, and Washington, DC.

Starting Out

Internships and clerkships are often good ways to gain experience and enter the law field. Like other patent lawyers, you may want to apply for a clerkship in the U.S. Court of Appeals for the Federal Court in Washington, DC. To gain a clerkship, you should write to the judge while you are still in law school. Another option is to get a job at the U.S. Patent and Trademark Office. Finally, many people are recruited by law firms right out of law school. Your law school should have a placement office as well as offer you professional contacts through alumni that help you find a position.

Advancement

For biotechnology patent lawyers who excel at combining verbal and scientific skills, advancement can be rapid and exciting. It is not uncommon for lawyers with Ph.D.s in genetic engineering or related fields to find themselves flooded with clients. The most successful of these lawyers can hope to advance to partner positions at their firms or even to establish a sufficient client base with which to start their own firms.

Earnings

In the law field, salaries tend to increase in predictable increments as the lawyer gains in experience and seniority. According to the U.S. Department of Labor, the median annual income for all lawyers was $78,170 in 1998. Higher salaries are generally found at large firms with 75 or more lawyers. According to salary information from FindLaw (http://www.findlaw.com), a Web site that specializes in legal careers, first-year associates working at large firms in major cities generally earned between approximately $60,000 and $125,000 per year in 1999. Naturally, partners and shareholders can earn much more than this, from $140,000 to $250,000 or more per year.

Because of the advanced training required and the high stakes of the biotech industry, biotechnology patent attorneys tend to earn about $10,000 to $20,000 more a year than their peers at each rung of this ladder. For example, while a starting attorney may earn about $90,000, a starting biotechnology patent attorney would make as much as $110,000 or more. Other factors can also influence these numbers, however, including the degrees held by lawyers, the size of the firm, and the geographic location of the firm.

Work Environment

Generally, there is a heavy workload with this career, and stress is part of the job. Because there are still relatively few biotech patent lawyers, successful ones can find themselves in especially high demand, and keeping hours down to an even remotely reasonable number can be a challenge. However, even this negative aspect has its upside, since biotech patent lawyers entering the field in the next few years should find plenty of demand for their talents. Some travel may be involved in the work, and, of course, biotechnology patent lawyers must be able to work with a variety of people. In addition, these lawyers often have the benefit of having their intellectual curiosity satisfied by their work.

Outlook

Although the U.S. Department of Labor predicts employment for all lawyers to grow about as fast as the average through 2008, biotechnology patent attorneys will probably find that the demand for their services remains high over that period. Because the legislation allowing for the patenting of biological organisms has only been in existence since the early 1980s, the pool of trained biotech patent attorneys is still small. Currently, many of the practicing biotechnology patent attorneys came to the field as a second career once they had already obtained their scientific training. As Lawrence Foster points out, "It wasn't really until the mid-1990s that college students began to choose and pursue careers as biotechnology patent attorneys."

As with other law fields, the development of biotech patent law is closely tied to the development of the industry it supports. In recent years, many biotechnology corporations have begun merging with and buying out smaller companies, resulting in fewer and larger companies. If this development continues, more companies will be large enough to hire their own in-house counsels.

For More Information

For information on all areas of law, law schools, the bar exam, and career guidance, contact:

American Bar Association
541 North Fairbanks Court
Chicago, IL 60611
Tel: 312-988-5522
Web: http://www.abanet.org

For more information on the specialty of intellectual property law, contact:

American Intellectual Property Lawyers Association
2001 Jefferson Davis Highway, Suite 203
Arlington, VA 22202-3694
Tel: 703-415-0780
Web: http://www.aipla.org

To learn more about the U.S. Patent and Trademark Office, contact:

General Information Services Division
United States Patent and Trademark Office
Crystal Plaza 3, Room 2C02
Washington, DC 20231
Tel: 800-786-9199
Web: http://www.uspto.gov

For information on the LSAT and law schools, contact:

Law School Admission Council
PO Box 40
Newton, PA 18940
Tel: 215-968-1001
Web: http://www.lsac.org

For a wealth of information on legal subjects, careers, and law schools, check out the following Web site:

FindLaw
Web: http://www.findlaw.com

Botanists

School Subjects
Agriculture
Biology

Personal Skills
Helping/teaching
Technical/scientific

Work Environment
Indoors and outdoors
Primarily one location

Minimum Education Level
Bachelor's degree

Salary Range
$29,000 to $45,700 to $86,020+

Certification or Licensing
None available

Outlook
Faster than the average

Overview

Botanists study all different aspects of plant life: from cell structure to reproduction, to how plants are distributed, to how rainfall or other conditions affect them, and more. Botany is an integral part of modern science and industry, with diverse applications in agriculture, agronomy (soil and crop science), conservation, manufacturing, forestry, horticulture, and other areas. Botanists work for the government, in research and teaching institutions, and for private industry. The primary task of botanists is research and applied research. Nonresearch jobs in testing and inspection, or as lab technicians/technical assistants, also are available. Botany is an extremely diverse field with many specialties.

History

Plant science is hundreds of years old. The invention of microscopes in the 1600s was very important to the development of modern botany. Microscopes allowed minute study of plant anatomy and cells and led to considerable research in the field. It was in the 1600s that people started using words like "botanographist," or one who describes plants, and "botanologist," an early version of the word "botanist."

In the 1700s, Carolus Linnaeus (1707-78), a Swedish botanist and taxonomist (one who identifies, names, and classifies plants) was an important figure. He came up with the two-name (genus and species) system for describing plants that is still used today. In all, Linnaeus wrote more than 180 works on plants, plant diseases, and related subjects.

The first experiments in hybridization were done by a monk, Gregor Johann Mendel (1822-84), in Austria. Mendel experimented on garden peas and other plants to figure out why organisms inherit the traits they do. His work is the basis for 20th-century work in plant and animal genetics. As interest in botany grew, botanical gardens became popular in Europe and North America.

Botany is a major branch of biology; the other is zoology. Today, studies in botany reach into many areas of biology, including genetics, biophysics, and other specialized studies. It has taken on particular urgency as a potential source of help for creating new drugs to fight disease, meeting food needs of developing countries, and battling environmental problems.

The Job

Research and applied research are the primary tasks of botanists. Literally every aspect of plant life is studied: cell structure, anatomy, heredity, reproduction, and growth; how plants are distributed on the earth; how rainfall, climate, soil, elevation, and other conditions affect them; how humans can better use them. In most cases, botanists work at a specific problem or set of problems in their research. For example, they may develop new varieties of crops that will better resist disease. Some botanists focus on a specific type of plant species, such as fungi (mycology), or plants that are native to a specific area, such as a forest or prairie. A botanist working in private industry, for example for a food or drug company, may focus on new-product development, testing and inspection, regulatory compliance, or other areas.

Research takes place in laboratories, experiment stations (research sites that are found at many universities), botanical gardens, and other facilities. Powerful microscopes and special mounting, staining, and preserving techniques may be used in the research.

Some botanists, particularly those working in conservation or ecological areas, also go out into the field. They inventory species, help recreate lost or damaged ecosystems, or direct pollution cleanup efforts.

Nonresearch jobs in testing and inspection or as lab technicians/technical assistants for universities, museums, government agencies, parks, manufacturing companies, botanical gardens, and other facilities also are available.

Botany is an extremely diverse field with many specialties. *Ethnobotanists* study the use of plant life by a particular culture, people, or ethnic group to find medicinal uses of certain plants. Study of traditional Native American medicinal uses of plants is an example.

Forest ecologists focus on forest species and their habitats, such as forest wetlands. Related studies include forest genetics and forest economics. Jobs in forestry include work in managing, maintaining, and improving forest species and environments.

Mycologists study fungi and apply their findings in agriculture, medicine, and industry for development of drugs, medicines, molds, and yeasts. They may specialize in research and development in such fields as antibiotics.

Toxicologists study the effect of toxic substances on organisms, including plants. Results of their work may be used in regulatory action, product labeling, and other areas.

Other botanical specialists include *pteridologists,* who study ferns and other related plants; *bryologists,* who study mosses and similar plants; and *lichenologists,* who study lichens, which are dual organisms made of both alga and fungus.

Requirements

High School

To prepare for a career in botany, high school students can explore their interests by taking biology, doing science projects involving plants, and working during summers or school holidays for a nursery, park, or similar operation. College prep courses in chemistry, physics, biology, mathematics, English, and foreign language are a good idea because educational requirements for professional botanists are high. Nonresearch jobs (test and inspection professionals, lab technicians, technical assistants) require at least a bachelor's degree in a biological science or botany; research and teaching positions usually require at least a master's or even a doctorate.

Postsecondary Training

At the undergraduate level, there are numerous programs for degrees in botany or biology (which includes studies in both botany and zoology). The master's level and above usually involves a specialized degree. One newer degree is conservation biology, which focuses on the conservation of specific plant and animal communities. The University of Wisconsin has one of the biggest programs in this area. Another key school is Yale's forestry school, which offers degrees in areas, such as natural resource management.

Other Requirements

Botanists become botanists because of their love for plants, gardening, and nature. They need patience, an exploring spirit, the ability to work well alone or with other people, good writing and other communication skills, and tenacity.

Exploring

The Botanical Society of America (BSA) suggests high school students take part in science fairs and clubs and get summer jobs with parks, nurseries, farms, experiment stations (research sites found at many universities), labs, camps, florists, or landscape architects. Hobbies like camping, photography, and computers are useful, too. Tour a botanical garden in your area and talk to staff. You can also get information by contacting national associations. For example, write to the BSA for a booklet on careers in botany.

Employers

Botanists find employment in the government, in research and teaching institutions, and in private industry. Local, state, and federal agencies, including the Department of Agriculture, Environmental Protection Agency, Public Health Service, National Biological Service, and even NASA employ botanists. Countless colleges and universities have botany departments and conduct botanical research. In private industry, botanists work for agribusiness, biotechnology, biological supply, chemical, environmental, food, lumber and paper, pharmaceutical, and petrochemical companies. Botanists also work for greenhouses, arboretums, herbariums, seed and nursery companies, fruit growers, and others.

Starting Out

With a bachelor's degree, a botanist's first job may be as a technical assistant or technician for a lab. Those with a master's degree might get work on a university research project. Someone with a doctorate might get into research and development with a drug, pharmaceutical, or other manufacturer.

For some positions, contract work might be necessary before the botanist gains a full-time position. Contract work is work done on a per-project, or freelance, basis: you sign on for that one project, and then you move on. Conservation groups like The Nature Conservancy hire hundreds of contract workers, including ecologists and botanists, each year to do certain work. Contract workers are especially in demand in the summer when there's a lot of biology inventory work to be done.

Opportunities for internships or volunteer positions are available with local chapters of The Nature Conservancy or the Student Conservation Association. (See end of article for contact information.) Land trusts are also good places to check for volunteer work.

Advancement

Federal employees generally move up the ranks after gaining a certain number of hours of experience and obtaining advanced degrees. The Botanical Society of America, whose membership primarily comes from universities, says keys for advancing in university positions include producing quality research, publishing a lot, and obtaining advanced degrees. Advancing in the private sector depends on the individual employer. Whatever the botanist can do to contribute to the bottom line, such as making breakthroughs in new-product development, improving growing methods, and creating better test and inspection methods, will probably help the botanist advance in the company.

Earnings

According to the National Association of Colleges and Employers, graduates with bachelor's degrees in biological science in 1999 generally started out earning $29,000 per year. Those with master's degrees in biological science averaged beginning salaries of $34,450; those with doctoral degrees averaged $45,700 as a starting salary. The U.S. Department of Labor reported that in 1998 the top 10 percent of biological scientists earned $86,020 or more.

At times, research botanists deeply involved with a project put in a lot of overtime. In exchange, they may be able to work fewer hours other weeks, depending on the specific employer. Botanists performing fieldwork also might have some flexibility of hours. In private industry, the workweek is likely to be a standard 35 to 40 hours. Benefits vary but usually include paid holidays and vacations, health insurance, and the like.

Work Environment

Botanists work in a wide variety of settings, some of them very pleasant— greenhouses, botanical gardens, or herbariums, for example. A botanist working for an environmental consultant or conservation organization may spend a lot of time outdoors, rain or shine. Some botanists interact with the public, such as in a public park or greenhouse, sharing their enthusiasm for the field. Other botanists spend their days in a lab, poring over specimens and writing up the results of their research.

As scientists, botanists need to be focused, patient, and determined. Some research spans many hours and even years of work. A botanist needs to believe in what he or she is doing and keep at a project until it's completed satisfactorily. The ability to work on one's own is important, but few scientists work in a vacuum. They cooperate with others, share the results of their work orally and in writing, and, particularly in private industry, they may need to explain what they're doing in layman's terms.

Because educational requirements for botanists are high, and because so much of the work involves research, it is important to be a good scholar and enjoy digging for answers.

Outlook

Average to faster-than-average growth in botany positions is expected through 2008. Botanists will be needed to help meet growing environmental, conservation, pharmaceutical, and similar demands. Government employment opportunities should stay strong, too, but will depend in part on the continued health of the national economy. Federal budget cuts may jeopardize some projects and positions. In general, however, botanists can expect to be in demand in a wide variety of fields. Experts say the outlook is best for those with an advanced degree.

For More Information

For the booklets, Careers in Botany *and* Botany for the Next Millennium, *contact:*

Botanical Society of America
1735 Neil Avenue
Columbus, OH 43210-1293
Tel: 614-292-3519
Email: bsa-manager@botany.org
Web: http://www.botany.org

For information on school and internship programs, news on endangered species, and becoming a member, contact or check out the following Web site:

National Wildlife Federation
11100 Wildlife Center Drive
Reston, VA 20190-5362
Tel: 800-822-9919
Web: http://www.nwf.org

For information about internships with state chapters or at headquarters, contact:

The Nature Conservancy
4245 North Fairfax Drive, Suite 100
Arlington, VA 22203-1606
Tel: 800-628-6860
Email: comment@tnc.org
Web: http://nature.org

To learn about volunteer positions in natural resource management, contact:

Student Conservation Association
PO Box 550
Charlestown, NH 03603
Tel: 603-543-1700
Web: http://www.sca-inc.org

This government agency manages more than 450 national wildlife refuges. For more information, contact:

U.S. Fish and Wildlife Service
U.S. Department of the Interior
1849 C Street, NW
Washington, DC 20240
Tel: 202-208-5634
Email: contact@fws.gov
Web: http://www.fws.gov

Cytotechnologists

Biology Chemistry	School Subjects
Helping/teaching Technical/scientific	Personal Skills
Primarily indoors Primarily one location	Work Environment
Bachelor's degree	Minimum Education Level
$19,400 to $32,440 to $48,300+	Salary Range
Required by certain states	Certification or Licensing
About as fast as the average	Outlook

Overview

Cytotechnologists are laboratory specialists who study cells under microscopes, searching for cell abnormalities such as changes in color, shape, or size that might indicate the presence of disease. Cytotechnologists may also assist physicians in the collection of body cells from various body sites, prepare slides, keep records, file reports, and consult with co-workers and pathologists. Most cytotechnologists work in private medical laboratories or in the laboratories of hospitals or research institutions.

History

The cytotechnology field is only a half-century old. It began in the 1940s, more than 10 years after Dr. George N. Papanicolaou (1883-1962), a Greek-American physician, developed a procedure for early diagnosis of cancer of the cervix in 1928, now known as the "Pap smear." This test involved collecting cell samples by scraping the cervixes of female patients, placing them on a glass slide, staining them, and examining them under a microscope to detect cell differences and abnormalities. As the value of the test became more widely accepted, the demand for trained personnel to read the Pap smears grew, and the career of cytotechnologist was born. This field has expanded to include the examination of other cell specimens.

The Job

Cytotechnologists primarily examine prepared slides of body cells by viewing them through a microscope. In any single slide there may be more than one hundred thousand cells so it is important that cytotechnologists be patient, thorough, and accurate when performing their job. They are required to study the slides and examine cell growth patterns, looking for abnormal patterns or changes in a cell's color, shape, or size that might indicate the presence of disease.

While most cytotechnologists spend the majority of their workday in the laboratory, some might assist doctors at patients' bedsides collecting cell samples from the respiratory and urinary systems as well as the gastrointestinal tract. They might also assist physicians with bronchoscopes and with needle aspirations, a process that uses very fine needles to suction cells from many locations within the body. Once the cells are collected, cytotechnologists may prepare the slides for microscope examination. In some laboratories, cell preparation is done by medical technicians known as *cytotechnicians*.

Cytotechnologists are often responsible for keeping records and filing reports. Although they usually work independently in the lab, they often share lab space and must consult with co-workers, supervisors, and pathologists regarding their findings. Most cytotechnologists work for private firms that are hired by physicians to evaluate medical tests, but they may also work for hospitals or university research institutions.

Requirements

High School

Biology, chemistry, and other science courses are essential if you want to become a cytotechnologist. In addition, math, English and computer literacy classes are also important. You should also take the courses necessary to fulfill the entrance requirements of the college or university you plan to attend.

Postsecondary Training

There are two options to becoming a cytotechnologist. The first involves earning a bachelor's degree in biology, life sciences, or a related field, then entering a one-year, postbaccalaureate certificate program offered by an accredited hospital or university.

The second option involves transferring into a cytotechnology program during your junior or senior year of college. Students on this track earn a bachelor of science degree in cytotechnology. In both cases, you would earn a college degree and complete at least one year of training devoted to cytotechnology.

The courses you will take include chemistry, biology, and math. Some programs also require their students to take business and computer classes as well.

Certification or Licensing

Cytotechnology graduates (from either degree programs or certificate programs) may register for the certification examination given by the Board of Registry of the American Society of Clinical Pathologists. Most states require cytotechnologists to be certified, and most employers insist that new employees be certified. Certification is usually a requirement for advancement in the field.

A number of states also require that personnel working in laboratories be licensed. It will be necessary for you to check the licensing requirements of the state in which you hope to work. The state's department of health or board of occupational licensing can provide you with this information.

It is important that practicing cytotechnologists remain current with new ideas, techniques, and medical discoveries. Many continuing-education programs are offered to help the professional remain current in the field of cytotechnology.

Other Requirements

If you wish to enter the field of cytotechnology you should be detail-oriented, a good observer, and able to make decisions. You should enjoy working alone, but you must also have the ability to work as a team member. It is essential that you are able to follow directions and have the ability to concentrate. Good writing, reporting, and organizational skills are also important. Cytotechnologists are often expected to sit at a stationary laboratory bench for long periods of time.

Employers

The majority of cytotechnologists are employed by private medical laboratories hired by physicians to evaluate medical tests. Others work for hospitals, nursing homes, public health facilities, or university research institutions, while some may be employed by federal and state governments.

Starting Out

Some universities and teaching hospitals have internship programs that can result in job offers upon graduation. Recruiters often visit universities and teaching hospitals in the months prior to a graduation in an effort to recruit cytotechnologists. Professional journals and large metropolitan newspapers often have classified ads that list opportunities for employment. Many university and teaching hospitals have a placement service that helps their graduates obtain employment upon graduation.

Advancement

Some cytotechnologists who work in larger labs may advance to supervisory positions. This type of advancement may be limited in smaller labs, however. Entering the teaching field and directing classes or supervising research may be another career advancement move. Some experienced cytotechnologists, along with other medical personnel, have opened their own laboratories. Obtaining additional education or training can open the door to other careers in the medical field.

Earnings

The U.S. Department of Labor reported the median yearly income of clinical laboratory technologists (including cytotechnologists) to be $32,440 in 1998. The lowest paid 10 percent, which typically includes those just beginning in the field, earned around $19,400. The highest paid 10 percent made approximately $48,300 or more.

Salaries are determined by the experience and education of the cytotechnologist and by the type of employer. Generally, federal government employees are paid a lower salary, while cytotechnologists working in private laboratories earn slightly more than those working in hospitals. Salaries tend to be higher in the West.

Benefits such as vacation time, sick leave, insurance, and other fringe benefits vary by employer, but are usually consistent with other full-time health care workers.

Work Environment

Cytotechnologists usually work independently in a well-lighted laboratory examining slides under the microscope. Often this involves sitting at a workstation for a considerable length of time and requires intense concentration. Some cytotechnologists might assist other medical personnel with the direct collection of cell samples from patients. This type of work requires interfacing directly with people who are ill or who may be concerned about their health and the test results.

Daily schedules and shifts may vary according to the size of the laboratory and medical facility.

Outlook

Competition to enter cytotechnology programs is keen, and there is also keen competition among graduates for jobs. The U.S. Department of Labor predicts employment for this group to grow about as fast as the average through 2008. Advances in technology have made many new diagnostic tests possible, but advances in technology have also caused much automation to take place in the laboratory. So, while there are new tests for the cytotechnologist to perform, there are also fewer old tests that need the cytotechnologist's expert handling. However, it is important to note that government regulations currently limit the number of slides cytotechnologists may work with each day, adding to demand in this field.

For More Information

For information on cytotechnology careers, accredited schools, and employment opportunities, contact the following organizations:

American Society for Cytopathology
400 West 9th Street, Suite 201
Wilmington, DE 19801
Tel: 302-429-8802
Email: asc@cytopathology.org
Web: http://www.cytopathology.org

American Society for Cytotechnology
1500 Sunday Drive, Suite 102
Raleigh, NC 27607
Tel: 800-948-3947
Email: info@asct.com
Web: http://www.asct.com

American Society of Clinical Pathologists
2100 West Harrison Street
Chicago, IL 60612
Tel: 312-738-1336
Email: info@ascp.org
Web: http://www.ascp.org/

Commission on Accreditation of Allied Health Education Programs
35 East Wacker Drive, Suite 1970
Chicago, IL 60601-2208
Tel: 312-553-9355
Email: caahep@caahep.org
Web: http://www.caahep.org/

Ecologists

School Subjects	Biology Chemistry
Personal Skills	Communication/ideas Technical/scientific
Work Environment	Primarily outdoors Primarily multiple locations
Minimum Education Level	Bachelor's degree
Salary Range	$24,000 to $46,140 to $91,000+
Certification or Licensing	None available
Outlook	Faster than the average

Overview

Ecology is the study of the interconnections between organisms (plants, animals) and the physical environment. It links biology, which includes both zoology (the study of animals) and botany (the study of plants), with physical sciences, such as geology and paleontology. Thus, *ecologist* is a broad job title for any of a number of different biological or physical scientists concerned with the study of plants or animals within their environment.

History

Much of the science that ecologists use is not new. The ancient Greeks recorded their observations of natural history many centuries ago. However, linking together the studies of life and the physical environment is fairly new. The term "ecology" was first defined in 1866 by Ernst von Haeckel (1834-1919), a German biologist. Like many scientists of his time, he grappled with Charles Darwin's (1809-82) theory of evolution based on natural selection. This theory said that those species of plants and animals that were best adapted to their environment would survive. Although Haeckel did not agree with Darwin, he and many other scientists grew fascinated with the links between living things and their physical environment. At that time, very important discoveries in geology proved that many forms of plants and animals had once existed but had died out. Fossils showed startlingly unfamiliar plant types, for example, as well as prehistoric animal remains that no one had ever imagined existed. (Before such discoveries, people assumed that the species they saw all around them had always existed.) Realization that there were important connections between living things and their physical environment was a key step in the development of the science of ecology.

Like most of the other environmental careers, the professional field of ecology did not really grow popular until the late 1960s and early 1970s. Before then, some scientists and others had tried to warn the public about the ill effects of industrialization, unchecked natural resource consumption, overpopulation, spoiling of wilderness areas, and other thoughtless misuse of the environment. But not until the years after World War II—with growing use of radiation and of pesticides and other chemicals, soaring industrial and automobile pollution, and increasing discharge into waterways—did widespread public alarm about the environment grow. By this time, many feared it was too late. Heavy municipal and industrial discharge into Lake Erie, for example, made it unable to sustain life as before.

In response, the U.S. government passed a series of hard-hitting environmental laws through the 1960s and 1970s. To become compliant with these laws, companies and municipalities began to look around for professionals who understood the problems and could help take steps to remedy them. Originally, they drew professionals from many existing fields, such as geologists, sanitary engineers, biologists, chemists, and others. These professionals may not have studied environmental problems as such at school, but they were able to apply the science they knew to the problems at hand.

To some extent, this continues to be true today. Many people working on environmental problems still come out of general science or engineering backgrounds. Recently, however, there has been a trend toward specialization. Students in many fields—from biology and chemistry to engineering, law, urban planning, communications, and others—can obtain degrees with specialization in the environment. An ecologist today can either have a background in traditional biological or physical sciences or have studied these subjects specifically in the context of environmental problems.

The Job

The main unit of study in ecology is the ecosystem. Ecosystems are communities of plants and animals within a given habitat that provide the necessary means of survival, including food and water. Ecosystems are defined by such physical conditions as climate, altitude, latitude, soil and water characteristics, and so forth. Examples include forests, tundra, savannas (grasslands), and rainforests, among others.

There are many complex and delicate interrelationships within an ecosystem. For example, green plants use the energy of sunlight to make carbohydrates, fats, and proteins; some animals eat these plants and acquire part of the energy of the carbohydrates, fats, and proteins; other animals eat these animals and acquire a smaller part of that energy. Cycles of photosynthesis, respiration, and nitrogen fixation continuously recycle the chemicals of life needed to support the ecosystem. Anything that disrupts these cycles, from droughts to air or water pollution, can disrupt the delicate workings of the entire ecosystem.

Therefore, a primary concern of ecologists today is to study and attempt to find solutions for disruptions in various ecosystems. Increasingly, an area of expertise is the reconstruction of ecosystems—that is, the re-creation of ecosystems that are destroyed or almost completely destroyed because of pollution, overuse of land, or other action.

According to the Environmental Careers Organization, a key area of work for ecologists is in land and water conservation. They help to restore damaged land and water as well as to preserve wild areas for the future. Understanding the links between organisms and their physical environments can be invaluable in such efforts.

Let's take an example to see how this works. Imagine that there is a large pond at the edge of a town. A woman out jogging one day notices that hundreds of small, dead fish have washed up at the edge of the pond, a "fish kill," in environmental language. Clearly, something is wrong: but what? A nearby factory discharges its wastewater into the pond. Is there something new in the wastewater that killed the fish? Or did something else kill the fish? A professional who understands the fish, the habitat (the pond), the possible reasons for the fish kill, and the potential solutions clearly would be useful here.

This is also true for environmental planning and resource management. Planning involves studying and reporting the impact of an action on the environment. For example, how might the construction of a new federal highway affect the surrounding ecosystem? A planning team may go to the site to view the physical geography and environment, the plants, and the animals. It also may recommend alternative actions that will have less damaging effects.

Resource management means determining what resources already exist and working to use them wisely. Professionals may build databases cataloging the plants, animals, and physical characteristics of a given area. They also may report on what can be done to ensure that the ecosystem can continue to sustain itself in the future. If an ecosystem has been completely destroyed, ecologists can help reconstruct it, getting the physical environment back up to par and reintroducing the species that used to live there.

Ecologists work in many areas of specialization. *Limnologists* study freshwater ecology; *hydrogeologists* focus on water on or below the surface of the earth; *paleontologists* study the remains of ancient life-forms in the form of fossils; *geomorphologists* study the origin of landforms and their changes; and *geochemists* study the chemistry of the earth, including the effect of pollution on the earth's chemistry. Other specialties are those of the endangered species biologists and wetlands ecologists.

Requirements

High School

If you are interested in becoming an ecologist, you should take science, biology, earth science, English, and math courses in high school.

Postsecondary Training

A bachelor of science degree is the minimum degree required for nonresearch jobs, which include testing and inspection. A master's degree is necessary for jobs in applied research or management. A Ph.D. generally is required to advance in the field, including into administrative positions.

The Environmental Careers Organization suggests that if you can only take one undergraduate major, it should be in the basic sciences: biology, botany, zoology, chemistry, physics, or geology. At the master's degree level, natural resource management, ecology, botany, conservation biology, and forestry studies are useful.

Other Requirements

Ecologists should appreciate and respect nature, and they must also be well versed in scientific fundamentals. Ecologists frequently, but not always, are naturally idealistic. They should be able to work with other people on a team and to express their special knowledge to the other people on the team, who may have different areas of specialization.

Exploring

You can seek more information about ecology from guidance counselors and professional ecologists who work at nearby colleges, universities, and government agencies. An easy way for you to learn more about ecology is to study your own environment. Trips to a nearby pond, forest, or park over the course of several months will provide opportunities to observe and collect data. Science teachers and local park service or arboretum personnel can also offer you guidance.

Employers

By far, the majority of land and water conservation jobs—about 75 percent—are in the public sector, according to the Environmental Careers Organization. This includes the federal government, the largest employer The Bureau of Land Management, the U.S. Fish and Wildlife Service, the National Park Service, and the U.S. Geological Service are among the federal agencies that manage U.S. conservation. Other public sector opportunities are with states, regions, and towns. Opportunities in the private sector can be found with utilities, timber companies, and consulting firms. An additional area of employment is in teaching.

Starting Out

You should volunteer with such groups as the Student Conservation Association (SCA), which places people in resource management projects. Programs include three- to five-week summer internships for high school students. If you have already graduated from high school (and are over age 18), you can check with SCA for internships in forest, wildlife, resource, and other agencies.

Another option is to contact a federal or local government agency directly about an internship. Many, including the Environmental Protection Agency, the National Park Service, and the Bureau of Land Management, have internship programs. Programs are more informal at the local level.

As for the private sector, an internship with a nonprofit organization may be possible. Such groups include the National Wildlife Federation and the Natural Resources Defense Council.

Entry-level ecologists also may take advantage of temporary or seasonal jobs to gain experience and establish crucial contacts in the field.

Advancement

Midlevel biological scientists may move to managerial positions within biology or to nontechnical administrative, sales, or managerial jobs. Ecologists with a Ph.D. may conduct independent research, advance into administrative positions, or teach on the college level, advancing from assistant professor to associate and tenured professorships.

Earnings

Salaries for ecologists vary depending on such factors as their level of education, experience, area of specialization, and the organization for which they work. For example, job postings for June 2000 on the Ecological Society of America's Web site listed a visiting instructor position at a college offering an annual salary of $24,000. The Web site also listed an opening for an experienced research plant physiologist with the U.S. Forest Service that would pay $59,623 to $91,589, depending on the person's experience. In 1998, the U.S. Department of Labor reported the median annual income of biological scientists, which includes ecologists, was $46,140. The lowest paid 10 percent of this group earned approximately $27,930 or less, while the highest paid 10 percent earned roughly $86,020 or more per year.

Federal agency jobs tend to pay more than state or local agency jobs. Private sector jobs tend to pay more than public sector jobs.

Work Environment

Ecologists can work in a variety of places, from wilderness areas to forests to mountain streams. Ecologists also might work in sewage treatment plants, spend their days in front of computers or in research laboratories, or find themselves testifying in court. A certain amount of idealism probably is useful, though not required. It takes more than just loving nature to be in this field; a person has to be good at scientific fundamentals. Ecologists might start out in the field collecting samples, making notes about animal habits, or doing other monitoring. They may need to be able to work as part of a team and express what they know in terms that everyone on the team can understand.

Outlook

Environmentally oriented jobs are expected to increase at a faster rate than the average for all occupations through 2008, according to the U.S. Department of Labor. Land and resource conservation jobs tend to be the most scarce, however, because of high popularity and tight budgets for agencies. Those with advanced degrees will fare better than ecologists with only bachelor's degrees.

For More Information

For information on careers in the geosciences, contact:

American Geological Institute
4220 King Street
Alexandria, VA 22302-1502
Tel: 703-379-2480
Web: http://www.agiweb.org

ESA offers a wide variety of publications, including Careers in Ecology, *which provides an overview of career possibilities, and* Issues in Ecology, *which discusses major ecology issues. For more information, contact:*

Ecological Society of America (ESA)
1707 H Street, NW, Suite 400
Washington, DC 20006
Tel: 202-833-8773
Email: esahq@esa.org
Web: http://esa.sdsc.edu

For information on internships, job opportunities, and student chapters, contact:

National Wildlife Federation
11100 Wildlife Center Drive
Reston, VA 20190-5362
Tel: 800-822-9919
Web: http://www.nwf.org

For information on student volunteer activities and programs, contact:

Student Conservation Association
PO Box 550
Charlestown, NH 03603
Tel: 603-543-1700
Email: cwcmail@sca-inc.org
Web: http://www.sca-inc.org

Food Technologists

Chemistry Mathematics	School Subjects
Following instructions Technical/scientific	Personal Skills
Primarily indoors Primarily one location	Work Environment
Bachelor's degree	Minimum Education Level
$20,000 to $42,340 to $200,000	Salary Range
Voluntary	Certification or Licensing
About as fast as the average	Outlook

Overview

Food technologists, sometimes known as *food scientists,* study the physical, chemical, and biological composition of food. They develop methods for safely processing, preserving, and packaging food and search for ways to improve its flavor and nutritional value. They also conduct tests to ensure that products, from fresh produce to packaged meals, meet industry and government standards.

History

One of the earliest methods of food preservation was drying. Grains were sun- and air-dried to prevent mold growth and insect damage. Fruits and vegetables dried in the sun and meats dried and smoked over a fire were stored for use during times of need. Fruits were preserved by fermenting them into wines and vinegars, and fermented milk became curds, cheeses, and yogurts.

Methods of food preservation improved over the centuries, but there were severe limitations until the evolution of scientific methods made it possible to preserve food. By creating conditions unfavorable to the growth or survival of spoilage microorganisms and preventing deterioration by enzymes, scientists were able to extend the storage life of foods well beyond the normal period.

For most of history, people bought or traded for bulk foods, such as grain or rice, rather than prepared foods. This began to change in the early 1800s, when new methods of preserving and packaging foods were developed. The science of food technology did not, however, really develop until shortly before the American entrance into World War II. Prompted by the need to supply U.S. troops with nutritious, flavorful foods that were not only easy to transport but also kept for long periods of time, scientists around 1940 began making great advances in the preparation, preservation, and packaging of foods. By the 1950s, food science and food technology departments were being established by many universities, and food science disciplines became important and respected areas of study.

Another boost to the food technology program came with the U.S. space program; new types of foods, as well as new types of preparation, packaging, and processing were needed to feed astronauts in space.

By the late 20th century, few people still canned or preserved their own fruits and vegetables. Advances in production methods in this century have made it possible to process larger quantities of a wider range of food products. Scientists specializing in food technology have found better ways to retard spoilage, improve flavor, and provide foods that are consistent in quality, flavor, texture, and size. Innovations such as freeze drying, irradiation, and artificial coloring and flavoring have changed the way many of the foods we eat are processed and prepared. Consumer demand for an ever-increasing variety of foods has created a demand for food technologists to develop them. Foods processed in a variety of ways are readily available to the consumer and have become such an accepted part of modern life that one rarely gives a thought to the complexities involved. The safety of the process, nutrition, development of new products and production methods, and the packaging of products are all the responsibility of food technologists.

The Job

Food technologists usually specialize in one phase of food technology. About one-third are involved in research and development. A large number are employed in quality-control laboratories or in the production or processing areas of food plants. Others teach or perform basic research in colleges and universities, work in sales or management positions, or are employed as technical writers or consultants. The branches of food technology are numerous and include cereal grains, meat and poultry, fats and oils, seafood, animal foods, beverages, dairy products, flavors, sugar and starches, stabilizers, preservatives, colors, and nutritional additives.

Food technologists in basic research study the structure and composition of food and observe the changes that take place during storage or processing. The knowledge they gain may enable them to develop new sources of proteins, determine the effects of processing on microorganisms, or isolate factors that affect the flavor, appearance, or texture of foods. Technologists engaged in applied research and development have the more practical task of creating new food products and developing new processing methods. They also continue to work with existing foods to make them more nutritious and flavorful and to improve their color and texture.

A rapidly growing area of food technology is biotechnology. Food technologists in this area work with plant breeding, gene splicing, microbial fermentation, and plant cell tissue cultures to produce enhanced raw products for processing.

Foods may lose their characteristics and nutritious value during processing and storage. Food technologists seek ways to prevent this by developing improved methods for processing, production, quality control, packaging, and distribution. They conduct chemical and microbiological tests on products to be sure they conform to standards set by the government and by the food industry. They also determine the nutritive content (the amounts of sugar, starch, protein, fat, vitamins, and minerals) that federal regulations say must be printed on the labels.

Food technologists in quality-control laboratories concentrate on ensuring that foods in every stage of processing meet industry and government standards. They check to see that raw ingredients are fresh, sufficiently ripe, and suitable for processing. They conduct periodic inspections of processing line operations. They also test after processing to be sure that various enzymes are not active and that bacteria levels are low enough so the food will not spoil or be unsafe to eat.

Some technologists test new products in test kitchens or develop new processing methods in laboratory pilot plants. Others devise new methods for packaging and storing foods. To solve problems, they may confer with processing engineers, flavor experts, or packaging and marketing specialists.

In processing plants, food technologists are responsible for preparing production specifications and scheduling processing operations. They ensure that proper temperature and humidity levels are maintained in storage areas and that wastes are disposed of properly and other sanitary regulations are observed throughout the plant. They also make recommendations to management in matters relating to efficiency or economy, such as new equipment or suppliers.

Some food technologists have positions in other fields where they can apply their specialized knowledge to such areas as advertising, market research, or technical sales.

Requirements

High School

Students in high school can prepare for a technologist career by taking courses in biology, chemistry, physics, and mathematics, along with other college-preparatory courses.

Postsecondary Training

Educational requirements for this field are high. Beginners need at least a bachelor's degree in food technology. Some technologists hold degrees in other areas, such as chemistry, biology, engineering, agriculture, or business, and nearly half have advanced degrees. Master's degrees and doctorates are mandatory for college teaching and are usually necessary for management and research positions.

Undergraduate programs in food technology are offered by approximately 60 colleges and universities. Courses include physics, biochemistry, mathematics, microbiology, the social sciences and humanities, and business administration, in addition to food technology courses such as food preservation, processing, sanitation, and marketing. Most of these schools also offer advanced degrees, usually in specialized areas of food technology. To successfully complete their program, candidates for a master's degree or a doctoral degree must perform extensive research and write a thesis reporting their original findings. Specialists in administrative, managerial, or regulatory areas may earn advanced degrees in business administration or in law rather than in food technology.

Other Requirements

Food technologists should have analytical minds and enjoy technical work. In addition, they must be able to express themselves clearly and be detail oriented. They also must be able to work well in group situations and participate and contribute to a team effort.

Exploring

Students may be able to arrange field trips to local food processing plants and plan interviews with or lectures by experts in the field. Apart from an interest in science, and especially chemistry, the prospective food technologist may also develop an interest in cooking and in inventing their own recipes.

Because of the educational requirements for food technologists, it is not likely that students will be able to acquire actual experience while still in high school. Part-time and summer employment as workers in food processing plants, however, would provide an excellent overview of the industry. More advanced college students may have opportunities for jobs helping out in research laboratories.

Employers

Food technologists work in a wide variety of settings, including food processing plants, food ingredient plants, and food manufacturing plants. They may work in basic research, product development, processing and quality assurance, packaging, or market research. There are positions in laboratories, test kitchens, and on production lines as well as with government agencies.

Starting Out

Many schools offering degree programs in food science will also offer job placement assistance. Also, recruiters from private industry frequently conduct interviews on campus. Faculty members may be willing to grant referrals to exceptional students. Another method is to make direct application to individual companies.

Frequently, the food products with which food technologists work determine where they are employed. Those who work with meats or grains may work in the Midwest. Technologists who work with citrus fruits usually work in Florida or California. Two-thirds of all food technologists are employed by private industry. The remaining work for the federal government. Some major government employers of food technologists include the Environmental Protection Agency, NASA, the Food and Drug Administration, and the U.S. Department of Agriculture.

Advancement

For food technologists with a bachelor's degree, there are two general paths to advancement, depending on whether they work in production or in research. They may begin as quality-assurance chemists or assistant production managers and, with experience, move up to more responsible management positions. Some technologists may start as junior food chemists in the research and development laboratory of a food company and advance to section head or another research management position.

Technologists who hold master's degrees may start out as food chemists in a research and development laboratory. Those with doctorates usually begin their careers in basic research or teaching. Other food technologists may gain expertise in more specialized areas and become sensory evaluation experts or food-marketing specialists.

Earnings

Salaries for food technologists range from $20,000 to $200,000. According to the *Occupational Outlook Handbook,* median annual earnings of agricultural and food scientists were $42,340 in 1998.

Beginning food technologists with a bachelor's degree in food science or a related discipline average about $29,300 per year. With experience, food technologists earn about $47,000 per year. Those with advanced degrees can earn considerably more. The average salary for food technologists holding a master's degree in science is about $51,000 per year. Food technologists with doctoral degrees earn over $65,000 per year, while those with an M.B.A. degree can earn $75,000 per year or more.

Food technologists with a bachelor's degree who work for the federal government earn starting salaries that range from $19,700 to $26,700 a year. After several years of employment, government food technologists may earn between $35,000 and $50,000 a year.

Food technologist salaries vary somewhat depending on the region where they work. Those in the South Atlantic and Pacific states generally earn the highest salaries, while those in the West South Central states of Texas, Oklahoma, Arkansas, and Louisiana earn the lowest salaries. However, the cost of living in a particular area plays a role in the level of a food technologist's salary.

Most food technologists will receive generous benefit plans, which usually include health insurance, life insurance, pension plans, and vacation and sick pay. Others may receive funds for continuing education.

Work Environment

Most food technologists work regular hours in clean, well-lighted, temperature controlled offices, laboratories, or classrooms. Technologists in production and quality-control work in processing plants may be subject to machine noise and hot or cold conditions.

Outlook

The food industry is the largest single industry in the United States and throughout the world. There are roughly 70,000 food technologists employed in the United States. Because people have to eat, there will always be a need for people to develop, test, and process food products. In developed countries, the ever-present consumer demand for new and different food products means that the outlook for food scientists and technologists is very good.

Several factors have also increased the demand for skilled technologists. New labeling laws enacted in the 1990s have required companies to provide detailed nutritional information on their products. The continuing trend toward more healthful eating habits has recently focused on the roles of fats, cholesterol, and salt in nutrition, and companies have rushed to create a variety of low-fat, low-sodium, fat-free, cholesterol-free, and sodium-free foods. A larger and more varied supply of wholesome and economical food is needed to satisfy current tastes. The food industry will have to produce convenience foods of greater quality for use in homes and for the food service institutions that supply airlines, restaurants, and other major customers. More technologists may be hired to research and produce new foods from modifications of wheat, corn, rice, and soybeans, such as the "meat" products made from vegetable proteins. The food industry has increased its spending in recent years for this kind of research and development and is likely to continue to do so. Developing these products, without sacrificing such important factors as taste, appearance, and texture, has produced many new opportunities for food technologists.

Food technologists will also be sought to produce new foods for poor and starving people in underdeveloped countries. Experienced technologists will use their advanced training to create new foods from such "staples" as rice, corn, wheat, and soybeans.

Finally, the increasing emphasis on the automation of many elements of food processing has also created a need for food technologists to adapt cooking and preparation processes to the new technology.

For More Information

For information on accredited educational programs in food science and career publications, contact:

Institute of Food Technologists
221 North LaSalle Street, Suite 300
Chicago, IL 60601-1291
Tel: 312-782-8424
Web: http://www.ift.org/

For additional information, contact the following organizations:

National Food Processors Association
1350 I Street, NW, Suite 300
Washington, DC 20005
Tel: 202-639-5900
Web: http://www.nfpa-food.org/

U.S. Department of Agriculture
14th Street and Independence Avenue, SW
Washington, DC 20250
Web: http://www.usda.gov/

Forensic Experts

School Subjects
Biology
Chemistry

Personal Skills
Following instructions
Technical/scientific

Work Environment
Primarily indoors
Primarily multiple locations

Minimum Education Level
Bachelor's degree

Salary Range
$20,000 to $50,000 to $100,000+

Certification or Licensing
None available

Outlook
More slowly than the average

Overview

Forensic experts apply scientific principles and methods to the analysis, identification, and classification of physical evidence relating to criminal (or suspected criminal) cases. They do much of their work in laboratories, where they subject evidence to tests and then record the results. They may travel to crime scenes to collect evidence and record the physical facts of the site. Forensic experts may also be called upon to testify as expert witnesses and to present scientific findings in court.

History

In Scotland during the late 1780s, a man was convicted of murder when the soles of his boots matched a plaster cast of footprints taken from the scene of the crime. This is one of the earliest recorded cases of the use of physical evidence to link a suspected criminal with the crime.

In the late 19th century, scientists learned to analyze and classify poisons so their presence could be traced in a body. At about the same time, a controversy arose over the different methods being used to identify individuals positively. Fingerprinting emerged in the early 20th century as the most reliable method of personal identification. With the advent of X-ray technology, experts could rely on dental records to substitute for fingerprint analysis when a corpse was in advanced stages of decomposition and the condition of the skin had deteriorated.

Forensic pathology (medical examination of suspicious or unexplained deaths) also came into prominence at this time, as did ballistics, which is the study of projectiles and how they are shot from firearms. The study of ballistics was aided by the invention of the comparison microscope, which enabled an investigator to look at bullets side by side and compare their individual markings. Since individual gun barrels "scar" bullets in a unique pattern, similar markings found on different bullets may prove that they were fired from the same weapon.

These investigations by pioneer forensic scientists led the courts and the police to acknowledge the value of scientifically examined physical evidence in establishing guilt or innocence, confirming identity, proving authenticity of documents, and establishing cause of death. As the result of this acceptance by the legal and law enforcement communities, crime laboratories were established. One of the first, largest, and most complete laboratories is that of the Federal Bureau of Investigation (FBI), founded in 1932. Today, the FBI laboratory examines many thousands of pieces of evidence each year, and its employees present their findings in trials all over the United States and around the world. As the forensic sciences proved their worth, crime laboratories were established in larger cities and by state police departments. These laboratories are used in turn by many communities too small to support labs of their own. The scientific analysis of evidence has become an accepted part of police procedure, and new forensic advances, such as DNA testing, are being developed every day.

The Job

Forensic experts, also called *criminalists,* use the instruments of science and engineering to examine physical evidence. They use spectroscopes, microscopes, gas chromatographs, infrared and ultraviolet light, microphotography, and other lab measuring and testing equipment to analyze fibers, fabric, dust, soils, paint chips, glass fragments, fire accelerants, paper and ink, and other substances in order to identify their composition and origin. They analyze poisons, drugs, and other substances found in bodies by examining tissue samples, stomach contents, and blood samples. They analyze and classify blood, blood alcohol, semen, hair, fingernails, teeth, human and animal bones and tissue, and other biological specimens. Using samples of the genetic material DNA, they can match a person with a sample of body tissue. They study documents to determine whether they are forged or genuine. They also examine the physical properties of firearms, bullets, and explosives.

At the scene of a crime (whether actual or suspected), forensic experts collect and label evidence. This painstaking task may involve searching for spent bullets or bits of an exploded bomb and other objects scattered by an explosion. They might look for footprints, fingerprints, and tire tracks that must be recorded or preserved by plaster casting before they are wiped out. Since crime scenes must eventually be cleaned up, forensic experts take notes and photographs to preserve the arrangement of objects, bodies, and debris. They are sometimes called on later to reconstruct the scene of a crime by making a floor plan or map that shows the exact location of bodies, weapons, and furniture.

One important discipline within forensic science is identification. *Fingerprint classifiers* catalog and compare fingerprints of suspected criminals with records to determine if the people who left the fingerprints at the scene of a crime were involved in previous crimes. They often try to match the fingerprints of unknown corpses with fingerprint records to establish their identity. They work in laboratories and offices, as well as travel to other areas such as crime scenes. Retrieving fingerprints outside may be difficult and require specialized processes, such as dusting glassware, windows, or walls with a fine powder. This powder contrasts with many different surfaces and will highlight any fingerprints that remain. Another method of retrieving fingerprints is to lift them off with a flexible tape, which can be brought back to the laboratory for further evaluation and matching.

Fingerprint classifiers compare new prints against those found after the commission of similar crimes. The classifier documents this information and transfers it to the main record-keeping system, often a large mainframe computer system. In the last decade or so, computers have greatly enhanced the possibility of matching new fingerprints to those already on file. A fingerprint classifier may keep individual files on current crimes and note any similarities between them.

Identification technicians work at various jobs related to maintaining police records. In addition to handling fingerprint records, they also work with other kinds of records, such as police reports and eyewitness information about crimes and accidents. They operate equipment used to microfilm police records, as well as store the microfilm and retrieve or copy records upon the request of police or other public officials. *Forensic pathologists* perform autopsies to determine the cause of death; autopsies are almost always performed on victims of crime. *Forensic psychiatrists* also conduct psychiatric evaluations of accused criminals and are often called to testify on whether the accused is mentally fit to stand trial.

Molecular biologists and *geneticists* analyze and review forensic and paternity samples, provide expert testimony in civil and criminal trials, and identify and develop new technologies for use in human identification.

Other job titles within forensic science include *forensic toxicologists,* who are concerned with detecting and identifying the presence of poisons or drugs in a victim's body; *forensic odontologists,* who use dental records and evidence to identify crime victims and to investigate bite marks; and *forensic anthropologists,* who examine and identify bones and skeletal remains.

Forensic experts spend the bulk of their time in the laboratory working with physical evidence. They seldom have direct contact with persons involved in actual or suspected crimes or with police investigators except when collecting evidence and reporting findings. Forensic experts do not interpret their findings relative to the criminal investigation in which they are involved; that is the work of police investigators. The purpose of crime lab work is to provide reliable scientific analysis of evidence that can then be used in criminal investigations and, if needed later, in court proceedings.

Requirements

High School

Almost all jobs in this field require at least a bachelor's degree. In high school, you can begin to prepare for this field by taking a heavy concentration of science courses, including chemistry, biology, physiology, and physics. Computer skills are also important, especially for fingerprint classifiers. A basic grounding in spoken and written communications will be useful because forensic experts must write very detailed reports and are sometimes called on to present their findings in court.

Postsecondary Training

A number of universities and community colleges in the United States offer programs in forensic science, pathology, and various aspects of crime lab work. These courses are often spread throughout the school, in the anatomy, physiology, chemistry, or biology departments, or they may be grouped together as part of the criminal justice department.

Certification or Licensing

Certification may be an advantage for people working in toxicology and document examination. Specialists in these and other disciplines may also be required to take undergraduate and graduate course work in their areas. In a field such as toxicology, advanced chemistry work is important. The certificate programs are available through the Forensic Sciences Foundation, a branch of the American Academy of Forensic Sciences.

Other Requirements

To be successful in this field, you should have an aptitude for scientific investigation, an inquiring and logical mind, and the ability to make precise measurements and observations. Patience and persistence are important qualities, as is a good memory. Forensic experts must constantly bear in mind that the accuracy of their lab investigations can have great consequences for others.

Exploring

A large community police department may have a crime lab of its own whose experts can give you specific information about their work and the preparation that helped them build their careers. Smaller communities often use the lab facilities of a larger city nearby or the state police. A school counselor or a representative of the local police may be able to help you arrange a tour of these labs. Lectures in forensic science given at universities or police conventions may also be open to students. Online services and Internet access may provide entry to forums devoted to forensic science and are a good source of information on the daily and professional experiences of people already active in this field.

Employers

Forensic scientists are typically employed by large police departments or state or law enforcement agencies nationwide. However, certain disciplines are often self-employed or work in the private sector. For example, *forensic engineers,* who use mathematical principles to reconstruct accident scenes, determine the origins of explosions and fires, or review the design of chemical or molecular structures, may be employed by large corporations, small firms, or government agencies. Forensic anthropologists, who identify skeletal remains, may work within a university or college, teaching related courses, conducting research, and consulting on cases submitted by law enforcement agencies. They may also be employed by the military or a medical examiner's office. Many forensic science concentrations also offer part-time, or consulting, opportunities depending on the level of education and experience.

Starting Out

Crime labs are maintained by the federal government and by state and local governments. Applications should be made directly to the personnel department of the government agency supporting the lab. Civil service appointments usually require applicants to take an examination. Such appointments are usually widely advertised well in advance of the application date. Those working for the FBI or other law enforcement agencies usually undergo background checks that examine their character, background, previous employers, and family and friends.

Advancement

In a large crime laboratory, forensic technicians usually advance from an assistant's position to working independently at one or more special types of analysis. From there they may advance to a position as project leader or being in charge of all aspects of one particular investigation. In smaller labs, one technician may have to fill many roles. With experience, such a technician may progress to more responsible work but receive no advancement in title. Fingerprint classifiers who work for police departments may pursue advancement with a different government agency or apply for positions with the FBI.

Crucial to advancement is further education. Forensic experts need to be familiar with scientific procedures such as gas chromatography, ultraviolet and infrared spectrophotometry, mass spectroscopy, electrophoresis, polarizing microscopy, light microscopy, and conventional and isoelectric focusing; knowledge of these analytical techniques and procedures is taught or more fully explored at the master's and doctorate level. Other, more specific areas of forensics, such as DNA analysis, require advanced degrees in molecular biology and genetics.

Earnings

Earnings for forensic analysts vary with the employer, geographic location, and educational and skill level. Salaries for entry-level positions as research assistants or technicians working in local and regional labs range from $20,000 to $25,000. For those individuals with a bachelor's degree and two to five years of specialized experience, salaries range from $30,000 to $40,000. Salaries for those with advanced degrees range from $50,000 to well over $100,000 a year.

Work Environment

Forensic experts usually perform the analysis portion of their work in clean, quiet, air-conditioned laboratories, but they are frequently required to travel to crime scenes to collect evidence or study the site to understand more fully the evidence collected by detectives. When gathering evidence and analyzing it, forensic experts need to be able to concentrate, sometimes in crowded, noisy situations. For this reason, forensic experts must be adaptable and able to work in a variety of environments, including dangerous or unpleasant places.

Many crime scenes are grisly and may be extremely distressing for beginning workers and even for more seasoned professionals. In addition, forensic experts who work with human remains will regularly view corpses, and, more often than not, these corpses will have been mutilated in some way or be in varying degrees of decomposition. Individuals interested in this field need to develop the detachment and objectivity necessary to view corpses and extract specimens for testing and analysis.

Simulating the precise conditions of a crime site is often crucial, so forensic experts often return to the site, so that they can perform tests or functions outside of the controlled environment of their lab. When traveling to the scene of a crime, forensic experts may have to carry cases of tools, cameras, and chemicals. In order not to risk contaminating evidence, they must follow strict procedures (both in and out of the laboratory) for collecting and testing evidence; these procedures can be extremely time-consuming and thus require a great deal of patience. Forensic experts also need to be able to arrive at and present their findings impartially. In large labs, they often work as part of a team under the direction of a senior technologist. They may experience eyestrain and contact with strong chemicals, but little heavy physical work is involved.

Outlook

The number of forensic experts employed in the United States is expected to grow more slowly than the average for all other occupations over the next decade, according to the U.S. Department of Labor. This is a small career group, numbering only a few thousand (not including the many scientific experts who are called in as consultants when their expertise is needed). Population increases, a rising crime rate, and the greater emphasis on scientific methodology in crime investigation, however, will likely increase the need for trained experts. While some government agencies may be under pressure to reduce staff because of budget problems, the number of forensic experts is expected to show some growth through the next decade.

For More Information

For information on certification, careers, and colleges and universities that offer forensic science programs, contact:

American Academy of Forensic Sciences
PO Box 669
Colorado Springs, CO 80901-0669
Tel: 719-636-1100
Web: http://www.aafs.org/

For the career kit, **FBI Career Opportunities,** *contact:*

> **Federal Bureau of Investigation**
> J. Edgar Hoover Building
> 935 Pennsylvania Avenue, NW
> Washington, DC 20535
> Tel: 202-324-3000
> Web: http://www.fbi.gov

For additional career information, contact the following organizations:

> **American Society of Questioned Document Examiners**
> PO Box 382684
> Germantown, TN 38183-2684
> Tel: 901-759-0729
> Web: http://www.asqde.org/

> **Society of Forensic Toxicologists**
> PO Box 5543
> Mesa, AZ 85211-5543
> Tel: 480-839-9106
> Web: http://www.soft-tox.org/

Genetic Scientists

Biology Chemistry	School Subjects
Communication/ideas Technical/scientific	Personal Skills
Primarily indoors Primarily one location	Work Environment
Bachelor's degree	Minimum Education Level
$21,947 to $55,000 to $80,000+	Salary Range
None available	Certification or Licensing
Much faster than the average	Outlook

Overview

Genetic scientists, or *geneticists,* study heredity. They study plants as well as animals, including humans. Geneticists conduct research on how characteristics are passed from one generation to the next through the genes present in each cell of an organism. This research often involves manipulating or altering particular genetic characteristics to better understand how genetic systems work. For instance, genetic scientists may breed a family of mice with a tendency toward high blood pressure to test the effects of exercise or diet on that condition. Their work adds to the body of biological knowledge and helps prevent inheritable diseases. Genetics is a component of just about every area of biology and can be found in many biology subfields. Rapidly growing specialty areas include the fields of genetic counseling and medical genetics, and the role of genetics in medicine.

History

In the 1860s, an Austrian monk named Gregor Mendel (1822-84) discovered the principles of genetics by breeding different varieties of garden peas in his monastery garden. His experiments, which showed that crossing short and tall peas produced only tall plants rather than any of medium height, proved that no blending of traits occurred. Rather, tallness was the dominant (or more powerful) trait and shortness was recessive.

Fifty years after Mendel's discoveries, American biologist Thomas Hunt Morgan (1866-1945) discovered that genes are located on the chromosomes present in every cell. Genes are like a blueprint; they carry instructions for how an organism—human, animal, or plant—will be built. However, as Hugo de Vries (1848-1935) discovered in his research in the early 1900s, genes do not always copy themselves exactly. Sometimes they mutate, that is, change their blueprint from one generation to the next. Mutations are often responsible for illness.

The modern history of genetics began in the early 1950s with James Watson's and Francis Crick's discovery of the double helix, or spiral ladder, structure of DNA. Their discovery touched off a flurry of scientific activity that led to a better understanding of DNA chemistry and the genetic code. Before 1975, however, the technology for actually altering the genes of organisms for study or practical use was severely limited. For while the 1950s and 1960s saw big successes in gene transfer and molecular biology for the smaller and simpler bacteria cells, more complex organisms were another story. Even though both plant and animal cells could be grown in culture, the detailed workings of their genes remained a mystery until the discovery of recombinant DNA techniques. Recombinant DNA refers to combining the DNA, or genetic material, from two separate organisms to form unique DNA molecules that carry a new combination of genes. The major tools of this technology—and the second most important discovery in the field of genetics—are restriction enzymes, first discovered in the 1960s. They work by cutting up DNA molecules at particular points so that DNA pieces from different sources may be joined. These genetically engineered cells may then be cloned, or grown in culture, to make copies of the desired gene. The cloning of genetically engineered cells has many potentially useful applications for society, such as producing pest-resistant plants, altering bacteria for waste cleanup, or generating proteins for medical uses like dissolving blood clots or making human growth hormone.

The most ambitious project in DNA research to date made possible by advanced technology was the effort to map the entire human genome, or all the genetic material in human beings. Called the Human Genome Project (HGP), it is considered more important to science history than either the splitting of the atom or the moon landing. The U.S. government launched the HGP in 1990, with the goal of completing the sequencing by 2005. In 1998, Celera Genomics Corporation (a for-profit company) announced that it would start its own sequencing project to compete with the HGP. By 2000 (four years ahead of schedule) both organizations had completed rough drafts of the human genome. Project results promise new scientific knowledge, medicines, and therapies that can be used to battle diseases such as AIDS, cancer, arthritis, and osteoporosis. Continuing advances in automation and electronics, including use of the latest computer software, will greatly promote project goals and increase our understanding of genetics.

The Job

The goal of genetic scientists is to increase biological knowledge so as to understand and cure genetic diseases; counsel families at risk of having children with genetic defects; and breed new crops and livestock, among other things. Most geneticists spend their time in a laboratory isolating particular genes in tissue samples and doing experiments to find out which characteristics those genes are responsible for. They work with chemicals, heat, light, and such instruments as microscopes, computers, electron microscopes, and other technical equipment. Besides having excellent mathematical and analytical skills, which will help them design and carry out experiments and analyze results, genetic scientists must also develop good writing and teaching techniques. They must be able to communicate their research results to students in classroom settings and to colleagues through published papers.

Profound academic and technological advances made over the last decade have brought about rapid progress in the field and opened up a whole new world for genetic scientists, who can now go just about anywhere their imagination leads them. Some of the many specialty areas for geneticists are described here.

Research geneticists typically complete a Ph.D. program, carrying out original research under a faculty member's direction. After earning their Ph.D.s, most graduates do research for two to four years as postdoctoral fellows. Following this training, they are then qualified to hold faculty positions at academic institutions or to join the staffs of research institutes or biotechnology firms. Jasper Rine, a genetics professor at the University of California, uses the courses he teaches as an excuse to keep himself up on the latest discoveries. He is currently studying the behavioral traits of purebred dogs, trying to figure out to what extent simple behaviors in dogs are inherited. His experiment involves mating a Newfoundland with a Border Collie and then studying the physical characteristics and behaviors of their puppies. Once they're old enough, the puppies will be mated to see what traits get passed through to a second generation. The idea is to try and identify specific genes in dogs that contribute to a particular behavior, like the Border Collie's strong herding instinct or the Newfoundland's natural instinct for water rescue (a Border Collie puppy will use a water bowl for drinking, while a Newfoundland puppy will try and swim in it!). Information from this research may help to identify genes that affect human behavior, also known to be strongly influenced by genetics.

Laboratory geneticists apply modern genetic technology to agriculture, police work, pharmaceutical development, and clinical medicine. They typically have four to six years of college and are part of a staff of scientists trained in molecular biology, cytogenetics, biochemical genetics, immunogenetics, and related disciplines. Some genetic laboratories require their staff members to have specific training and certification in cytogenetic or medical technology.

Some genetic scientists specialize as *genetic counselors.* They are health professionals with specialized graduate degrees in medical genetics and counseling. They work as a valuable part of a health care team, giving information and support to families with birth defects or genetic disorders. They also help individuals who themselves have genetic conditions and counsel couples concerned about passing a harmful gene to a child. Genetic counselors identify families at risk, take down family medical histories, and obtain and interpret information about genetic conditions. They perform blood tests to detect possible harmful genes and predict the likelihood of genetic diseases occurring in children. Genetic counselors run down available options with their clients, serving as patient advocates and making referrals to community or state support services. Some genetic counselors serve in administrative roles, while many conduct research activities related to the field of medical genetics and genetic counseling. One prominent genetic counselor, Joan Scott, who studies the molecular genetics of cancer at a commercial laboratory, calls genetic counseling "an intellectually stimulating field" that has allowed her to pursue several interests at once: working with families, teaching, writing, and research. She sees working with families as the most important part of her job, however.

Clinical geneticists are even more highly trained specialists in the genetics field. They are generally medical doctors, having received an M.D. degree and completed a pediatric, internal medicine, or obstetric residency, followed by specialized genetics training. Many clinical geneticists work at university medical centers or large hospitals, while some have private practices. Generally, this job involves recognizing genetic disorders and birth defects, understanding what they mean for the patient, arranging the proper treatment, and helping the patient and family understand and cope with the disorder. Some clinical geneticists work mainly with infants and children, while others may specialize in the genetic problems of babies still in the womb. They may also work with adult patients with inherited forms of heart disease, cancer, or neurological disease. An increasingly important role for the clinical geneticist is to be the link between scientists who are constantly advancing the field and the patients who stand to benefit from their discoveries. As Nancy Fisher, a clinical geneticist and medical director for the Medical Assistance Administration, Washington State Department of Social and Health Services, states, "Genetics is an exciting and ever-changing field. The explosion of knowledge in genetics is exhilarating. I am glad I am a geneticist and, moreover, I am definitely not bored!"

Cytogenetic technologists study chromosome structure and function. They analyze chromosomes by making them visible under light microscopy. Living cells are first treated with a special stain that reveals stripes of light and dark regions along the length of each chromosome. Because the stripes are highly specific for a particular chromosome, stripe patterns help differentiate chromosomes from one another, making any abnormalities in number easily seen. Chromosome analysis may be done on just about any living tissue, but for clinical work, it usually is done on amniotic fluid (fluid surrounding the fetus), chorionic villi (fetal placenta), blood, bone marrow, and miscarriages. The work is challenging, like piecing together a jigsaw puzzle. According to Mark Terry, a cytogenetic technologist working in a hospital cytogenetics lab, his job has been "a pleasant surprise," providing a wide range of challenges that include clinical work, research, technical writing, book reviews, and essay writing. "Unlike much clinical laboratory work," explains Terry, "it is not 'kit' oriented. We are allowed to experiment and expand the boundaries of the science, blending cell biology, tissue culture, cytogenetics, and molecular genetics to attempt to solve complex medical puzzles."

Molecular geneticists study DNA, the blueprint for protein molecules in cells. An offshoot of cytogenetics, forensic genetics, is used by the law enforcement community to perform DNA fingerprinting, a subspecialty that is currently booming. Alec Jeffreys, a professor at Leicester University, discovered that each of us has highly specific patterns within our DNA located on many different chromosomes. The pattern is so distinctive that no two people's are the same, except for identical twins, which is why the technique is called DNA fingerprinting. It has been used to identify and convict criminals and to determine parentage.

Genetic engineers experiment with altering, splicing, and rearranging genes for specific results. This research has resulted in the discovery and production of insulin and interferon, two medical breakthroughs that can treat genetically caused diseases like diabetes. Agricultural triumphs like hybrid corn, disease-resistant grains, and higher quality livestock are all products of the principles of recombinant DNA and cloning.

Another specialty area for geneticists is population genetics. *Population geneticists* examine the breeding methods of farm animals and crops. They look at mutations that occur spontaneously or are introduced purposely to produce a marketable result.

Requirements

High School

If you are interested in becoming a geneticist working in basic research, you should study math, chemistry, and physics in high school, along with biology. English, writing, and computer studies are helpful for developing communications skills. A college degree is a must.

Postsecondary Training

In college, students wishing to become basic research geneticists typically major in biology or genetics, taking math, chemistry, and physics courses as well. However, you could also major in any one of the physical sciences with a minor in biology and still enter graduate school in the field of genetics. At public and private universities, colleges, and medical schools, genetic scientists almost always hold doctoral degrees and teach undergraduate and graduate courses in addition to doing research. Clinical geneticists usually earn an M.D. degree, which requires getting admitted to medical school, then completing a three- to-five-year residency in a medical specialty followed by an additional two to three years of specialized training in genetics.

Career opportunities also exist for those with bachelor's or master's of science degrees, particularly in the rapidly growing biotechnology field, which is using genetics to produce everything from medicines to microchips. This industry needs well-trained research technicians who typically have a bachelor of science degree in biology with a molecular or biochemistry emphasis. The federal government also has a need for research technicians and hires college graduates and those with master's degrees to work in hospitals and U.S. Department of Agriculture laboratories. Cytogenetic technologists generally need a bachelor of science degree.

Genetic counselors usually hold specialized graduate degrees. Training programs for genetic counselors are two-year master's-level programs with courses and field training in medical genetics and counseling.

Certification or Licensing

Geneticists do not need to be licensed. However, those with clinical practices in human or medical genetics may get certification through both the American Board of Medical Genetics and the American Board of Genetic Counseling. Some genetic laboratories require staff to have specific training and certification in cytogenetic or medical technology, while others hire people with any relevant B.S. or M.S. degree as long as they show an aptitude for the work. Graduates of a master's degree program in genetic counseling can apply to sit for the certification examination of the American Board of Genetic Counseling.

Other Requirements

Geneticists must be smart and have inquiring minds. They need to be able to evaluate results and draw conclusions from measurable criteria. They should also be able to work with abstract theories and ideas, and in cooperation with others. Both written and verbal communications skills are important for sharing research information. Important personal qualities for laboratory scientists are patience, attention to detail, and determination. Genetic counselors must have mature judgment and strong communications skills to deal with people coping with highly emotional issues. They must be able to establish trust quickly and have the right mix of objectivity (the ability to be neutral) and sensitivity to do their work well.

Exploring

As a high school student, you can prepare for a career as a genetic scientist by taking as many courses in math and science as you can. You should also develop your writing and computer skills. High school science teachers can often contact departments of biology and genetics at nearby colleges and universities and arrange field trips or college speakers. Speakers can give you information about university summer programs. Take advantage of these and other opportunities offered in your community through community colleges, museums, professional associations, and special interest groups.

Employers

Genetic scientists work for a variety of employers, including biotechnology firms, research centers, government agencies, and agricultural stations and farms. Government laboratories that employ genetic scientists include the U.S. Department of Agriculture, the Fish and Wildlife Service, the National Institutes of Health, and several others. Genetic scientists are also needed by agricultural colleges seeking practical applications of genetics for livestock, poultry, or crops. Genetic scientists working in this setting divide their time between teaching and research programs. Most of these jobs are in college and university departments of biology, botany, zoology, or microbiology.

Starting Out

Because this career is such a broad one with many varied fields within it, methods of entry also vary, depending on the specialty area you choose. As early as high school, opportunities exist for paid and unpaid internships at a number of science laboratories. Job seekers can get leads from their professors or fellow students. You could join a team of researchers as a laboratory aide or technician.

If you are interested in a job with the federal government, contact a local Federal Job Information Office or regional Office of Personnel Management to find out which tests you need to take. Federal agencies also come to college campuses to recruit graduates. You can look up federal job openings in the biweekly bulletin, *Federal Career Opportunities,* available by subscription and at your local library, and apply directly to the federal agency or department you are interested in. You can also look up federal job openings online at http://www.fedjobs.com.

If you would like to work at a college or university after completing an advanced degree, you may wish to continue your education through a post-doctoral fellowship, assisting a prominent scientist with research. Colleges and universities advertise open positions in professional journals and in the *Chronicle of Higher Education,* available at public libraries. You should also consult pharmaceutical and biotechnology companies' departments of human resources for employment opportunities in those industries.

Advancement

At colleges and universities, beginning teachers and researchers are hired at the assistant professor level. With additional years of experience and an impressive level of published research and teaching, they are promoted to associate professor and then to full professor. Similar years of experience lead to promotion in private industry and government agencies. Promotion usually involves an increase in salary as well as more job duties and greater work prominence.

Earnings

The starting salary in 2001 for genetic scientists with a bachelor's degree who went to work for the federal government at the GS-5 entry level was $21,947. For those with a master's degree, who qualified to start at the GS-7 or GS-9 levels, the beginning salary was $27,185 and $33,254, respectively, in 2001. Doctoral degree holders who qualified to start at the GS-11 level earned $40,236 in 2001. The average salary for genetic scientists working in private industry is around $55,000, with biotechnology firms offering even higher salaries. The highest paid, most experienced genetic scientists make upwards of $70,000 to $80,000 a year. Universities, which generally hire only geneticists with doctoral degrees, offer starting salaries ranging from $31,000 for new assistant professors to $52,000 for full professors.

According to a member survey by the National Society of Genetic Counselors, genetic counselors earned annual salaries that ranged from $23,575 to $72,500 in 2000. The survey also reported the following 2000 mean earnings for genetic counselors by specialty: pediatrics, $42,935; prenatal, $45,582; cancer, $46,647; molecular/cytogenetic, $50,643; and specialty disease, $44,545.

Work Environment

Genetic scientists spend most of their time in laboratories, designing and conducting research experiments. Most of these experiments will take many hours and yield few publishable results. But while breakthrough discoveries occur rarely and often involve hours of repetitive work, they can result in patents and significant royalties, not to mention the payoff of lives saved or diseases eliminated. Even small discoveries in the genetics field add to biological knowledge and can often lead to elimination of disease. Genetic scientists also spend considerable time writing reports about their experiments, lecturing or teaching about their research, and preparing grant proposals to federal or private agencies to secure funding to support their research. Because federal grants are extremely competitive, only the best-written and most scientifically up-to-date proposals will receive funding. Therefore, genetic scientists must keep improving their skills and knowledge throughout their careers to keep up with new developments in the field and to advance their own research. Usually, geneticists work as part of a research team, cooperating on various aspects of their experiments. Geneticists often head up teams of researchers, graduate students, and laboratory personnel. They may work from nine to five, although they may be required to work late into the night and on weekends during critical periods of an experiment. They may also work extra hours to complete research projects, to write reports of findings, or to read the latest developments in their specialty. Like other life scientists, geneticists must study throughout their careers to keep up with new developments in the field and to advance their own research.

Outlook

Interest in the field of genetic research has exploded in the past decade, with breakthrough discoveries bringing greater attention to the exciting possibilities of finding genetic causes and cures for diseases. As a result, employment in the field is expected to grow at rate faster than the average for all occupations.

Working in an age with virtually no limits, geneticists have the luxury of choosing their focus according to what interests them most. Rapid progress in the field, along with new methods of mapping genetic traits, has put all natural variation in all organisms within the grasp of genetic investigators. It is estimated that every human disease that is caused by a single gene defect will be curable by genetic intervention during the lifetime of students currently in high school. As the need to understand human and animal biology and genetics and the fight to eradicate disease continue, demand for scientists will continue to increase. The world of criminal investigation is increasingly using genetics to win cases, drawing on genetic test results to identify culprits from a drop of blood. Genetics is also being used in food testing to detect the slightest contamination by disease-causing organisms.

Genetics clearly stands out as the field of the future. A survey conducted by the American Association for the Advancement of Science in 1992 asked its 2,500 members to name the scientific specialty with the most promise for the next decade. Genetics was listed as the number one choice by biologists, physicists and astronomers, social and behavioral scientists, and chemists. It was listed as the second most promising field by medical scientists, engineers, and earth scientists.

For More Information

For information about certification, contact the following organizations:

American Board of Genetic Counseling
9650 Rockville Pike
Bethesda, MD 20814-3998
Tel: 301-571-1825
Web: http://www.abgc.net/

American Board of Medical Genetics
9650 Rockville Pike
Bethesda, MD 20814-3998
Tel: 301-571-1825
Web: http://www.abmg.org/

For a list of graduate and postgraduate training programs in human genetics, contact:

American Society of Human Genetics
9650 Rockville Pike
Bethesda, MD 20814-3998
Tel: 301-571-1825
Web: http://www.faseb.org/genetics

For the career brochure, Solving the Puzzle: Careers in Genetics, *contact:*

Genetics Society of America
9650 Rockville Pike
Bethesda, MD 20814-3998
Tel: 301-571-1825
Web: http://www.faseb.org/genetics

For information on careers and a list of training programs, contact:

National Society of Genetic Counselors
233 Canterbury Drive
Wallingford, PA 19086
Tel: 610-872-7608
Email: nsgc@nsgc.org
Web: http://www.nsgc.org/

Marine Biologists

Biology Earth science	School Subjects
Mechanical/manipulative Technical/scientific	Personal Skills
Indoors and outdoors Primarily multiple locations	Work Environment
Bachelor's degree	Minimum Education Level
$21,000 to $36,000 to $100,000+	Salary Range
Required for certain positions	Certification or Licensing
About as fast as the average	Outlook

Overview

Marine biologists study species of plants and animals living in saltwater, their interactions with one another, and how they influence and are influenced by environmental factors. Marine biology is a branch of science, and biologists in this area work in myriad industries, including government agencies, universities, aquaria, and fish hatcheries, to name a few. They generally work either in a laboratory setting or in the field, which in this case means being in or on the ocean or its margins.

History

Marine biologists started to make their study into a real science around the 19th century with a series of British expeditions. In 1872, the HMS *Challenger* set sail with scientists like Sir Charles Wyville Thomson and Sir John Murray on the most important oceanographic mission of all time. Over four years, they traveled 69,000 miles and cataloged 4,717 new species of marine plants and animals. Many marine scientists view the reports from this expedition as the basis of modern oceanography.

Before this time, marine scientists believed that sea creatures inhabited only shallow waters. They believed that the intense cold, pressure, and darkness below about 1,800 feet could not support life. Then, in the late 1860s, the HMS *Lightning* and the HMS *Porcupine* made hauls from below 14,400 feet that contained bizarre new creatures.

Scientists began to build precision equipment for measuring oceanic conditions. Among these were thermometers that could gauge the temperature at any depth, containers that could be closed at a desired depth to collect seawater, and coring instruments used to sample bottom sediments. Scientists also figured out techniques for measuring levels of salt, oxygen, and nutrients right on board ship.

Twentieth-century innovations such as underwater cameras, oxygen tanks, submersible craft, and heavy-duty diving gear that can withstand extremes of cold and pressure have made it possible for biologists to observe sea creatures in their natural habitats.

The Job

Marine biologists study and work with sea creatures in their natural environment—the oceans of the world and tidal pools along shorelines—as well as in laboratories. These scientists are interested in knowing how the ocean's changing conditions, such as temperature and chemical pollutants, can affect the plants and animals that live there. For example, what happens when certain species become extinct or are no longer safe to be eaten? Marine biologists can begin to understand how the world's food supply is diminished and help come up with solutions that can change such problem situations.

The work of these scientists is also important for improving and controlling sport and commercial fishing. Through underwater exploration, marine biologists have discovered that the world's coral reefs are being damaged by humans; they have also charted the migration of whales and counted the decreasing numbers of certain species; they have observed dolphins being accidentally caught in tuna fishermen's nets. By writing reports and research papers about such discoveries, a marine biologist can inform others about problems that need attention and begin to make important changes that could help the world.

To study plants and animals, marine biologists spend some of their work time in the ocean wearing wetsuits to keep warm (because of the frigid temperature below the surface of the sea) and scuba gear to breathe underwater.

They gather specimens with a slurp gun, which sucks fish into a specimen bag without causing them injury. They must learn how to conduct their research without damaging the marine environment, which is delicate. Marine biologists must also face the threat to their own safety from dangerous fish and underwater conditions.

Marine biologists also study life in tidal pools along the shoreline. They might collect specimens at the same time of day for days at a time. They would keep samples from different pools separate and keep records of the pool's location and the types and measurements of the specimens taken. This ensures that the studies are as accurate as possible. After collecting specimens, they keep them in a portable aquarium tank on board ship. After returning to land, which may not be for weeks or months, marine biologists begin to study specimens in a laboratory, often with other people working on the same study. They might, for example, check the amount of oxygen in a sea turtle's bloodstream to learn how the turtles can stay underwater for so long; or measure the "antifreeze" in the blood of an arctic fish to discover how it can survive frigid temperatures.

Requirements

High School

High school students should take biology and other sciences such as earth sciences, computer science, and chemistry. Participation in science clubs will give you experience working on projects with a team.

Postsecondary Training

If you're interested in marine biology you should take basic science courses such as biology, botany, and chemistry. However, classes don't end there. For instance, in biology you might be required to choose from marine invertebrate biology, ecology, oceanography, genetics, animal physiology, plant physiology, and aquatic plant biology. You might also be required to choose several more specific classes from such choices as ichthyology, vertebrate structure, population biology, developmental biology, biology of microorganisms, evolution, and cell biology. Classes in other subjects will also be required, like computer science, math (including algebra, trigonometry, calculus, analytical geometry, and statistics), and physics.

Although it is possible to get a job as a marine biologist with just a bachelor's degree, most marine biologists have a master's or doctoral degree.

Certification or Licensing

If you are going to be diving, organizations like the Professional Association of Diving Instructors provide basic certification. Training for scientific diving is more in-depth and requires passing an exam. It is also critical that divers learn cardiopulmonary resuscitation (CPR) and first aid. Also, if you'll be handling hazardous materials in a lab such as formaldehyde, strong acids, or radioactive nucleotides, you must be licensed.

Other Requirements

You should have an ability to ask questions and solve problems, observe small details carefully, do research, and analyze mathematical information. You should be inquisitive and must think for yourself. This is essential to the scientific method. You must use your creative ability and be inventive in order to design experiments; these are the scientist's means of asking questions of the natural world. Working in the field often requires some strength and physical endurance, particularly if you are scuba diving or if you are doing fieldwork in tidepools, which can involve hiking over miles of shore at low tide, keeping your footing on weedy rocks, and lifting and turning stones to find specimens.

Exploring

Volunteering at a local aquarium is an excellent way to learn about marine life and about the life of a marine biologist.

You can begin diving training while in high school. Between the ages of 12 and 15 you can earn a Junior Open Water Diver certification, which allows you to dive in the company of a certified adult. At 15, you can upgrade your certification to Open Water Diver.

Employers

Employers in this field range from pharmaceutical companies researching marine sources for medicines to federal agencies that regulate marine fisheries, such as the fisheries division of the National Oceanographic and Atmospheric Association. Aquariums hire marine biologists to collect and study specimens.

After acquiring many years of experience, you might be eligible for a faculty position at a school like the Scripps Institute of Oceanography or the University of Washington.

Marine products companies, which manufacture carrageenan and agar (extracted from algae and used as thickening agents in foods), hire biologists to design and carry out research.

Jobs in marine biology are based mostly in coastal areas, though some biologists work inland as university professors, or perhaps as paleontologists who search for and study marine fossils.

Starting Out

With a bachelor's degree only, you may be able to get a job as a laboratory technician in a state or federal agency. Some aquaria will hire you straight out of college, but generally it's easier to get a paid position if you've worked as a volunteer at the aquarium. You'll need a more advanced degree to get into more technical positions such as consulting, writing for scientific journals, or conducting research.

Web sites are good resources for employment information. If you can find the human resources section of an aquarium's home page, it will tell you whom to contact to find out about openings and may even provide job listings. Federal agencies may also have Web sites with human resource information.

Professors who know you as a student might be able to help you locate a position, as they might have connections in the professional world.

Another good way to make contacts is by attending conferences or seminars sponsored by aquatic science organizations such as the American Society of Limnology and Oceanography or the Mid-Atlantic Marine Education Association.

Advancement

If you are a lab technician with a four-year degree, you may become a senior lab tech after years with the same lab. Generally, though, taking on greater responsibility or getting into more technical work means further education. If you want to do research in any setting, you'll need a graduate degree or at least be working on one. To get an administrative position with a marine products company or a faculty position at a university, you'll need at least a master's degree, and if you hope to become a senior scientist at a marine station or a full professor, you must have a doctoral degree.

Earnings

Salaries will vary quite a lot depending on level of education, type of work, size and location of the operation, and level of experience. Based on information from the American Society of Limnology and Oceanography, those with bachelor's degrees and no experience might find work with the federal government with a salary around $21,000 to $33,000. The average biologist earns about $36,000 yearly. However, those with doctoral degrees in marine biology or one of its subfields can earn as much as $80,000. Senior scientists and full professors at universities can make more than $100,000.

Work Environment

Most marine biologists don't actually spend a lot of time diving. However, researchers might spend a couple hours periodically breathing from a scuba tank below some waters, like Monterey Bay or the Gulf of Maine. They might gather samples from the deck of a large research vessel during a two-month expedition, or they might be sitting in a conference room with several other research biologists.

In most marine biology work, some portion of time is spent in the lab, analyzing samples of seawater or collating data on a computer. Many hours are spent in solitude, reading papers in scientific journals or writing papers for publication.

Instructors or professors work in classrooms interacting with students and directing student lab work.

Those who work for an aquarium, as consultants for private corporations, or in universities work an average of 40 to 50 hours a week.

Outlook

Generally speaking, there are more marine biologists than there are paying positions at present. Changes in the earth's environment, such as global warming and increased levels of heavy metals in the global water cycle, will most likely prompt more research and result in slightly more jobs in different subfields.

Greater need for smart management of the world's fisheries, research by pharmaceutical companies into deriving medicines from marine organisms, and cultivation of marine food alternatives such as seaweeds and plankton are other factors that may increase the demand for marine biologists in the near future.

For More Information

For information on careers, contact:

American Society of Limnology and Oceanography
5400 Bosque Boulevard, Suite 680
Waco, Texas 76710-4446
Web: http://www.aslo.org

For reference lists, links to marine labs, summer intern and course opportunities, and links to career information, check out the following Web site:

Marine Biology Web Page
State University of New York
Department of Ecology and Evolution
Stony Brook, New York 11794
Tel: 516-632-8602
Email: levinton@life.bio.sunysb.edu
Web: http://life.bio.sunysb.edu/marinebio/mbweb.html

For information on volunteer programs for in-state students and college intern-ships, contact:

National Aquarium in Baltimore
501 E. Pratt Street
Baltimore, MD 21210
Tel: 410-576-3800
Email: intern@aqua.org
Web: http://aqua.org

For information on diving instruction and certification, contact:

Professional Association of Diving Instructors
30151 Tomas Street
Rancho Santa Margarita, CA 92688-2125
Tel: 949-858-7234
Web: http://www.padi.com

This center for research and education in global science currently runs more than 300 research programs and uses a fleet of four ships to conduct expeditions over the entire globe. For more information, contact:

Scripps Institution of Oceanography
University of California, San Diego
8602 La Jolla Shores Drive
La Jolla, CA 92037-1508
Tel: 619-534-3624
Email: siocomm@sio.ucsd.edu
Web: http://www-sio.ucsd.edu/

Medical Laboratory Technicians

School Subjects
| Biology
| Chemistry

Personal Skills
| Helping/teaching
| Technical/scientific

Work Environment
| Primarily indoors
| Primarily one location

Minimum Education Level
| Some postsecondary training

Salary Range
| $19,380 to $31,664 to $40,300

Certification or Licensing
| Required by certain states

Outlook
| About as fast as the average

Overview

Medical laboratory technicians perform routine tests in medical laboratories. These tests help physicians and other professional medical personnel diagnose and treat disease. Technicians prepare samples of body tissue; perform laboratory tests, such as urinalysis and blood counts; and make chemical and biological analyses of cells, tissue, blood, or other body specimens. They usually work under the supervision of a medical technologist or a laboratory director. Medical laboratory technicians may work in many fields, or specialize in one specific medical area, such as cytology (the study of cells), hematology (blood), serology (body fluids), or histology (body tissue).

History

Medical laboratory technology shares many important milestones with the history of medicine itself. For instance, both fields can claim as their founder Aristotle, the father of biology and physiology. Some significant achievements include Jan Swammerdam's discovery of red blood corpuscles in 1658; Anton van Leeuwenhoek's observation of microorganisms through the microscope during the latter part of the 17th century; and the discoveries of Robert Koch and Louis Pasteur in bacteriology in the 1870s.

The valuable information gained through these efforts showed medical professionals many possibilities for therapy, especially in the medical specialties of bacteriology (the study of microorganisms in the human body), cytology, histology, and hematology. The growth of these medical specialties created a steadily increasing need for laboratory personnel.

Because of the great medical advances of the 20th century, physicians are even more dependent on laboratory procedures and personnel for assistance in diagnosing and treating disease. In the early part of this century, individual physicians often taught their assistants how to perform some of the laboratory procedures frequently employed in their practices. Because the quality of work done by these technicians varied considerably, many physicians and medical educators became concerned with the problem of ensuring that assistants did the highest quality work possible. In 1936, one of the first attempts was made to standardize the training programs for the preparation of skilled assistants, in that case, the training of medical technologists. Since then, the National Accrediting Agency for Clinical Laboratory Sciences, in association with the Committee on Allied Health Education and Accreditation of the American Medical Association (CAHEA), has instituted standards of training for medical laboratory technicians. CAHEA has accredited more than one hundred educational programs offered in community, junior, and technical colleges for the training of medical laboratory technicians, and other accrediting agencies have also entered the field. For example, the Accrediting Bureau of Health Education Schools accredits education programs for medical laboratory technicians and medical assistants. In addition, CAHEA and other agencies have accredited dozens of additional programs for students willing to concentrate their studies in a medical laboratory specialty such as cytology, histology, or blood bank technology.

The Job

Medical laboratory technicians may be generalists in the field of laboratory technology; that is, they may be trained to carry out many different kinds of medical laboratory work. Alternatively, they may specialize in one type of medical laboratory work, such as cytology, hematology, blood bank technology, serology, or histology.

Medical laboratory technicians who work as *generalists* perform a wide variety of tests and laboratory procedures in chemistry, hematology (the study of blood, especially on the cellular level), urinalysis, blood banking, serology (the study and identification of antibodies found in the blood), and microbiology. By performing these tests and procedures, they help to develop vital data on the blood, tissues, and fluids of the human body. This data is then used by physicians, surgeons, pathologists, and other medical personnel to diagnose and treat patients.

The tests and procedures that these technicians perform are more complex than the routine duties assigned to laboratory assistants, but do not require specialized knowledge like those performed by more highly trained medical technologists. In general, medical laboratory technicians work with only limited supervision. This means that while the tests they perform may have well-established procedures, the technicians themselves must exercise independent judgment. For instance, they must be able to discriminate between very similar colors or shapes, correct their own errors using established strategies, and monitor ongoing quality control measures.

To carry out these responsibilities, medical laboratory technicians need a sound knowledge of specific techniques and instruments and must be able to recognize factors that potentially influence both the procedures they use and the results they obtain.

In their work, medical laboratory technicians frequently handle test tubes and other glassware and use precision equipment, such as microscopes and automated blood analyzers. (Blood analyzers determine the levels of certain blood components like cholesterol, sugar, and hemoglobin.) Technicians also are often responsible for making sure machines are functioning and supplies are adequately stocked.

Medical laboratory technicians who specialize in cytology are usually referred to as *cytotechnicians*. Cytotechnicians prepare and stain body cell samplings using special dyes that accentuate the delicate patterns of the cytoplasm, and structures such as the nucleus. Mounted on slides, the various features of the specimen then stand out brightly under a microscope. Using microscopes that magnify cells perhaps one thousand times, cytotechnicians screen out normal samplings and set aside those with minute irregularities (in cell size, shape, and color) for further study by a pathologist.

Medical laboratory technicians specializing in histology are usually referred to as *histologic technicians* or *tissue technicians*. Histology is the study of the structure and chemical composition of the tissues, and histologic technicians are mainly concerned with detecting tissue abnormalities and determining appropriate treatments for the disease conditions associated with the abnormalities.

Medical laboratory technicians who specialize in blood bank technology perform a wide variety of routine tests related to running blood banks, offering transfusion services, and investigating blood diseases and reactions to transfusions. Examples of tasks frequently performed by medical laboratory technicians specializing in this field include donor screening, determining blood types, performing tests of patients' blood counts, and assisting physicians in the care of patients with blood-related problems.

Most positions of responsibility in blood bank technology are held by certified specialists in Blood Bank Technology. To become certified in this field, a person needs a bachelor's degree and an additional year of training, which helps technicians become involved with research projects, teaching other health care workers, and supervising other employees.

Requirements

High School

To be hired as a medical laboratory technician, you must have a high school diploma and one or two years of postsecondary training. No specific kind of high school training is required; however, you must be able to meet the admissions requirements of institutions offering post-high school training. In general, courses in biology, chemistry, mathematics, English, and computer science are the ones that will be most helpful in a career as a medical laboratory technician.

Postsecondary Training

After high school, prospective technicians enroll in one- or two-year training programs accredited by the American Medical Association's Committee on Allied Health Education and Accreditation or the Accrediting Bureau of Health Education Schools. One-year programs include both classroom work and practical laboratory training and focus on areas such as medical ethics and conduct, medical terminology, basic laboratory solutions and media, manipulation of cytological and histological specimens, blood collecting techniques, and introductions to basic hematology, serology, blood banking, and urinalysis.

To earn an associate's degree, you must complete a two-year post-high school program. Like certificate programs, associate's degree programs include classroom instruction and practical training. Courses are taught both on-campus and in local hospitals. On-campus courses focus on general knowledge and basic skills in laboratory testing associated with hematology, serology, chemistry, microbiology, and other pertinent biological and medical areas. The clinical training program focuses on basic principles and skills required in medical diagnostic laboratory testing.

Certification or Licensing

Students who have earned an associate's degree are eligible for certification from several different agencies. You may become a certified medical laboratory technician by the Board of Registry of the American Society of Clinical Pathologists or the American Medical Technologists. The National Credentialing Agency for Laboratory Personnel offers certification to clinical laboratory technicians.

Prospective medical laboratory technicians who think they might want to specialize in cytology or blood bank technology should definitely consider the two-year program, which will best prepare them for the additional education they may need later.

In addition to completing the educational programs described above, prospective technicians need to pass an examination after graduation to receive certification. In some states, this certificate is all that is required for employment. In other states, state licensure is also required. School officials are the best source of information regarding state requirements.

Other Requirements

Besides fulfilling the academic requirements, medical laboratory technicians must have good manual dexterity, normal color vision, the ability to follow orders, and a tolerance for working under pressure.

Exploring

It is difficult for people interested in a career in medical laboratory technology to gain any direct experience through part-time employment. However, there are other ways to learn more about this career on a firsthand basis. Perhaps the best way is to arrange a visit to a hospital, blood bank, or commercial medical laboratory to see technicians at work at their jobs. Another way to learn about this kind of work in general, and about the training required in particular, is to visit an accredited school of medical laboratory technology to discuss career plans with the admissions counselor at the school. You can also write to the sources listed at the end of this article for more reading material on medical laboratory technology. Finally, students should remember that high school science courses with laboratory sections will give you exposure to some of the kinds of work you might do later in your careers.

Employers

Medical laboratory technicians are employed where physicians work, such as in hospitals, clinics, blood blanks, and commercial medical laboratories.

Starting Out

Graduates of medical laboratory technology schools usually receive assistance from faculty and school placement services to find their first jobs. Hospitals, laboratories, and other areas employing medical laboratory technicians may notify local schools of job openings. Often the hospital or laboratory at which you receive your practical training will offer full-time employment after graduation. Positions may also be secured using the various registries of certified medical laboratory workers. Newspaper job advertisements and commercial placement agencies are other sources of help in locating employment.

Advancement

Medical laboratory technicians often advance by returning to school to earn a bachelor's degree. This can lead to positions as medical technologists, histological technologists, cytotechnologists, or specialists in blood bank technology.

Other technicians advance by gaining more responsibility while retaining the title of technician. For instance, with experience, these workers can advance to supervisory positions or other positions assigning work to be done by other medical laboratory workers. Medical laboratory technicians may also advance by training to do very specialized or complex laboratory or research work.

Earnings

Salaries of medical laboratory technicians vary according to employer and geographical area. According to Salary.com, medical laboratory technicians earned a median base salary of $31,664 in May 2001. Fifty percent of workers in this field earn between $28,794 and $34,674 annually. The U.S. Department of Labor reported that in 1998 the lowest paid 10 percent of laboratory technologists and technicians, which typically includes those beginning in the field, earned approximately $19,380 per year. The department also recorded a median annual salary for all medical technologists and technicians of about $32,440 in 1998.

Medical laboratory technicians who go on to earn their bachelor's degrees and certification as medical technologists can expect an increase in annual earnings. According to the U.S. Department of Labor, the median annual salary for medical laboratory technologists working in hospitals was $36,500 in 1997. Those working in offices or clinics of medical doctors had a median salary of $40,300 that same year.

Most medical laboratory technicians receive paid vacations and holidays, sick leave, hospitalization and accident insurance, and retirement benefits.

Work Environment

Medical laboratory technicians work in clean, well-lighted, and usually air-conditioned settings. There may, however, be unpleasant odors and some infectious materials involved in the work. In general, there are few hazards associated with these odors and materials as long as proper methods of sterilization and handling of specimens, materials, and equipment are used.

Medical laboratory technicians often spend much of their days standing or sitting on stools. A 40-hour, five-day week is normal, although those working in hospitals can expect some evening and weekend work.

Medical laboratory technicians derive satisfaction from knowing their work is very important to patients and their physicians. Although the work involves new patient samples, it also involves some very repetitive tasks that some people may find trying. Additionally, the work must often be done under time pressure, even though it is often very painstaking.

Another factor that medical laboratory technicians should keep in mind is that advancement opportunities are limited, although they do exist. To maximize their chances for advancement, medical laboratory technicians must consider getting additional training.

Outlook

The U.S. Department of Labor predicts job growth for medical laboratory technicians to be about as fast as the average through 2008. Competition for jobs, however, may be strong. One reason for this increased competition is the overall national effort to control health care costs. Hospitals, where most medical laboratory technicians are employed, will seek to control costs in part through cutting down on the amount of laboratory testing they do and, consequently, the personnel they require.

Despite such cutbacks, though, the overall amount of medical laboratory testing will probably increase, as much of medical practice today relies on high-quality laboratory testing. However, because of the increased use of automation, this increase in laboratory testing will probably not lead to an equivalent growth in employment.

One other technological factor that will influence employment in this field is the development of laboratory-testing equipment that is easier to use. This means that some testing that formerly had to be done in hospitals or commercial laboratories can now be done in physicians' offices. This development may serve to slow growth in medical laboratory employment; however, it may increase the number of technicians hired by medical groups and clinics. In addition, equipment that is easier to use may also lead to technicians being able to do more kinds of testing, including some tests that used to be done only by medical technologists.

Despite these moderate growth projections, aspiring technicians should keep in mind that medical laboratory testing is an absolutely essential element in today's medicine. For well-trained technicians who are flexible in accepting responsibilities and willing to continue their education throughout their careers, employment opportunities should remain good.

For More Information

For information on careers, certification, and continuing education, contact the following organizations:

American Medical Association
515 North State Street
Chicago, IL 60610
Tel: 312-464-5000
Web: http://www.ama-assn.org

American Medical Technologists
710 Higgins Road
Park Ridge, IL 60068-5765
Tel: 847-823-5169
Email: amtmail@aol.com
Web: http://www.amt1.com

International Society for Clinical Laboratory Technology
818 Olive Street, Suite 918
St. Louis, MO 63101-1598
Tel: 314-241-1445

National Credentialing Agency for Laboratory Personnel
PO Box 15945-289
Lenexa, KS 66285
Tel: 913-438-5110
Email: nca-info@goamp.com
Web: http://www.nca-info.org

Naturalists

Overview

The primary role of *naturalists* is to educate the public about the environment and maintain the natural environment on land specifically dedicated to wilderness populations. Their primary responsibilities are preserving, restoring, maintaining, and protecting a natural habitat. Among the related responsibilities in these jobs are teaching, public speaking, writing, giving scientific and ecological demonstrations, and handling public relations and administrative tasks. Naturalists may work in a variety of environments, including private nature centers; local, state, and national parks and forests; wildlife museums; and independent nonprofit conservation and restoration associations. Some of the many job titles a naturalist might hold are wildlife manager, fish and game warden, fish and wildlife officer, land steward, wildlife biologist, and environmental interpreter. Natural resource managers, wildlife conservationists, and ecologists sometimes perform the work of naturalists.

History

Prior to the 17th century, there was little support for environmental preservation. Instead, wilderness was commonly seen as a vast resource to be controlled. This view began to change during the early years of the Industrial Revolution, when new energy resources were utilized, establishing an increasing need for petroleum, coal, natural gas, wood, and water for hydropowered energy. In England and France, for example, the rapid depletion of natural forests caused by the increased use of timber for powering the new industries led to demands for forest conservation.

The United States, especially during the 19th century, saw many of its great forests razed, huge tracts of land leveled for open-pit mining and quarrying, and increased disease with the rise of air pollution from the smokestacks of factories, home chimneys, and engine exhaust. Much of the land damage occurred at the same time as a dramatic depletion of wildlife, including elk, antelope, deer, bison, and other animals of the Great Plains. Some types of bear, cougar, and wolf became extinct, as did several kinds of birds, such as the passenger pigeon. In the latter half of the 19th century, the U.S. government set up a commission to develop scientific management of fisheries, established the first national park (Yellowstone National Park in Wyoming), and set aside the first forest reserves. The modern conservation movement grew out of these early steps.

States also established parks and forests for wilderness conservation. Parks and forests became places where people, especially urban dwellers, could acquaint themselves with the natural settings of their ancestors. Naturalists, employed by the government, institutions of higher education, and various private concerns, were involved not only in preserving and exploring the natural reserves but also in educating the public about the remaining wilderness.

Controversy over the proper role of U.S. parks and forests began soon after their creation (and continues to this day), as the value of these natural areas for logging, recreation, and other human activities conflicted with the ecological need for preservation. President Theodore Roosevelt, a strong supporter of the conservation movement, believed nevertheless in limited industrial projects, such as dams, within the wilderness areas. Despite the controversy, the system of national parks and forests expanded throughout the 20th century. Today, the Agriculture and Interior Departments, and, to a lesser extent, the Department of Defense, have conservation responsibilities for soil, forests, grasslands, water, wildlife, and federally owned land.

In the 1960s and early 1970s, the hazards posed by pollution to both humans and the environment highlighted the importance of nature preservation and public education. Federal agencies were established, such as the

Environmental Protection Agency, the Council on Environmental Quality, and the National Oceanic and Atmospheric Administration. Crucial legislation was passed, including the Wilderness Act (1964) and the Endangered Species Act (1969). Naturalists have been closely involved with these conservation efforts and others, shouldering the responsibility to communicate to the public the importance of maintaining diverse ecosystems and to help restore or balance ecosystems under threat.

The Job

Because of the impact of human populations on the environment, virtually no area in the United States is truly wild. Land and the animal populations require human intervention to help battle against the human encroachment that is damaging or hindering wildlife. Naturalists work to help wildlife maintain or improve their hold in the world.

The work can be directly involved in maintaining individual populations of animals or plants, overseeing whole ecosystems, or promoting the work of those who are directly involved in the maintenance of the ecosystem. *Fish and wildlife officers* (or *fish and game wardens*) work to preserve and restore the animal populations, including migratory birds that may only be part of the environment temporarily. *Wildlife managers, range managers,* and *conservationists* oversee the combination of plants and animals in their territories.

Fish and wildlife officers and wardens study, assist, and help regulate the populations of fish, hunted animals, and protected animals throughout the United States. They may work directly in the parks and reserves or they may oversee a region within a particular state, even if there are no park lands there. Fish and game wardens control the hunting and fishing of wild populations to make sure that the populations are not overharvested during a season. They monitor the populations of each species off season as well as make sure the species is thriving but is not overpopulating and running the risk of starvation or territory damage. Most people hear about the fish and game wardens when a population of animals has overgrown its territory and needs either to be culled (selectively hunted) or moved. Usually this occurs with the deer population, but it can also apply to predator animals such as the coyote or fox, or scavenger animals such as the raccoon. Because the practice of culling animal populations arouses controversy, the local press usually gives wide coverage to such situations.

The other common time to hear about wildlife wardens is when poaching is uncovered locally. Poaching can be hunting or fishing an animal out of season or hunting or fishing a protected animal. Although we think of poachers in the African plains hunting lions and elephants, poaching is common in the United States for animals such as mountain lions, brown bears, eagles, and wolves. Game wardens target and arrest poachers; punishment can include prison sentences and steep fines.

Wildlife managers, range managers, and conservationists work to maintain plant and animal life. Wildlife managers can work in local or national parks. Range managers work on ranges that have a combination of domestic and wild livestock. The U.S. government has permitted farmers to graze and raise livestock on federally held ranges, but this program is under increasing attack by conservationists. Range managers must ensure that both the domestic and wild populations are living side by side successfully. They make sure that the population of predatory wild animals does not increase enough to deplete the livestock and that the livestock does not overgraze the land and eliminate essential food for the wild animals. Range managers and conservationists must test soil and water for nutrients and pollution, count plant and animal populations in every season, and keep in contact with farmers using the land for reports of attacks on livestock or the presence of disease.

Wildlife managers also balance the needs of the humans using or traveling through the land they supervise and the animals that live in or travel through that same land. They keep track of the populations of animals and plants and provide food and water when it is lacking naturally. This may involve airdrops of hay and grain during winter months to deer, moose, or elk populations in remote reaches of a national forest or digging and filling a water reservoir for animals during a drought.

Naturalists in all these positions often have administrative duties such as supervising staff members and volunteers, raising funds (particularly for independent nonprofit organizations), writing grant applications, taking and keeping records and statistics, and maintaining public relations. They may write articles for local or national publications to inform and educate the public about their location or a specific project. They may be interviewed by journalists for reports concerning their site or their work.

Nature walks are often given to groups as a way of educating people about the land and the work that goes into revitalizing and maintaining it. Tourists, schoolchildren, amateur conservationists and naturalists, social clubs, and retirees commonly attend these walks. On a nature walk, the naturalist may point out specific plants and animals, identify rocks, and discuss soil composition or the natural history of the area (including special environmental strengths and problems). The naturalist may even discuss the indigenous people of the area, especially in terms of how they adapted to the unique aspects of their particular environment. Because such a variety of topics may be brought up, the naturalist must be an *environmental generalist,* familiar with such subjects as biology, botany, geology, geography, meteorology, anthropology, and history.

Naturalists educate the public about the environment through demonstrations, exhibits, and classes. For example, to help children understand oil spills, the naturalist may set up a demonstration showing that oil and water will not mix. Sometimes the natural setting will provides its own exhibit. Dead fish, birds, and other animals found in a park may help demonstrate the natural life cycle and the process of decomposition. Instruction may also be given on outdoor activities, such as hiking and camping.

For some naturalists, preparing educational materials is a large part of their job. Brochures, fact sheets, pamphlets, and newsletters may be written for people visiting the park or nature center. Materials might also be sent to area residents in an effort to gain public support.

One aspect of protecting any natural area involves communicating facts and debunking myths about how to respect the area and the flora and fauna that inhabit it. Another aspect involves tending managed areas to promote a diversity of plants and animals. This may mean introducing trails and footpaths that provide easy yet noninvasive access for the public; it may mean cordoning off an area to prevent foot traffic from ruining a patch of rare moss; or it may mean instigating a letter-writing campaign to drum up support for legislation to protect a specific area, plant, or animal. It may be easy to get support for protecting the snowshoe rabbit; it is harder to make the public understand the need to preserve and maintain a batcave.

Some naturalists, such as directors of nature centers or conservation organizations, have massive administrative responsibilities. They might recruit volunteers and supervise staff, organize long- and short-term program goals, and handle record-keeping and the budget. To raise money, naturalists may need to speak publicly on a regular basis, write grant proposals, and organize and attend scheduled fund-raising activities and community meetings. Naturalists also try to increase public awareness and support by writing press releases and organizing public workshops, conferences, seminars, meetings, and hearings. In general, naturalists must be available as resources for educating and advising the community.

Requirements

High School

High school students interested in the field should consider taking a number of basic science courses, including biology and chemistry. Botany courses and clubs are helpful, since they provide direct experience monitoring plant growth and health. Animal care experience, usually obtained through volunteer work, also is helpful.

Postsecondary Training

An undergraduate degree in environmental, physical, or natural sciences is generally the minimum educational requirement for becoming a naturalist. Common college majors are biology, forestry, wildlife management, natural resource and park management, natural resources, botany, zoology, chemistry, natural history, and environmental science. Course work in economics, history, anthropology, English, international studies, and communication arts are also helpful.

Graduate education is increasingly required for employment as a naturalist, particularly for upper level positions. A master's degree in natural science or natural resources is the minimum requirement for supervisory or administrative roles in many of the nonprofit agencies, and several positions require either a doctorate or several years of experience in the field. For positions in agencies with international sites, work abroad is necessary and can be obtained through volunteer positions such as those with the Peace Corps or in paid positions assisting in site administration and management.

Other Requirements

Those considering careers in this field should like working outdoors, as most naturalists spend the majority of their time outside in all kinds of weather. However, along with the desire to work in and with the natural world, the naturalist needs to be capable of communicating with the human world as well. Excellent writing skills are helpful in preparing educational materials and grant proposals.

For people working in the field, seemingly unrelated skills such as engine repair and basic carpentry can be essential to managing a post. Because of the remote locations of many of the work sites, self-sufficiency in operating and maintaining the equipment allows the staff to lose fewer days because of equipment breakdown.

Exploring

One of the best ways to learn about the job of a naturalist is to volunteer at one of the many national and state parks or nature centers. These institutions often recruit volunteers for outdoor work. College students, for example, are sometimes hired to work as summer or part-time nature guides. Outdoor recreation and training organizations, such as Outward Bound and the National Outdoor Leadership School, are especially good resources. Most volunteer positions, though, require a high school diploma and some college credit.

Students should also consider college internship programs. In addition, conservation programs and organizations throughout the country and the world offer opportunities for volunteer work in a wide variety of areas, including working with the public, giving lectures and guided tours, and working with others to build or maintain an ecosystem. For more frequent, up-to-date information, you can subscribe to one of several newsletters that post internship and job positions. *Environmental Careers World* (http://environmental-jobs.com) and *Environmental Career Opportunities* (http://eco-jobs.com/) are two online newsletters to look for.

Starting Out

For park employees, the usual method of entry is through part-time or seasonal employment for the first several jobs, then a full-time position. Because it is difficult to get experience before completing a college degree, and because seasonal employment is common, students interested in this career path should prepare to seek supplemental income for their first few years in the field.

International experience is helpful with agencies that work beyond the U.S. borders. This can be through the Peace Corps or other volunteer organizations that work with local populations on land and habitat management or restoration. Other volunteer experience is available through local restoration programs on sites in your area. Organizations such as the Nature Conservancy, Open Lands, and many others buy land to restore, and these organizations rely extensively on volunteer labor for stewarding and working the land. Rescue and release centers work with injured and abandoned wildlife to rehabilitate them. Opportunities at these centers can include banding wild animals for tracking, working with injured or adolescent animals for release training, and adapting unreleasable animals to educational programs and presentations.

Advancement

In some settings, such as small nature centers, there may be little room for advancement. In larger organizations, experience and additional education can lead to increased responsibility and pay. Among the higher-level positions is that of director, handling supervisory, administrative, and public relations tasks.

Advancement into upper-level management and supervisory positions usually requires a graduate degree, although people with a graduate degree and no work experience will still have to start in nearly entry-level positions. So you can either work a few years and then return to school to get an advanced degree or complete your education and start in the same position as you would have without the degree. The advanced degree will allow you eventually to move further up in the organizational structure.

Earnings

Starting salaries for full-time naturalists range from about $15,000 to $22,000 per year. Some part-time workers, however, make as little as minimum wage. For some positions, housing and vehicles may be provided. Earnings vary for those with added responsibilities or advanced degrees. Field officers and supervisors make between $25,000 and $45,000 a year, and upper management employees can make between $30,000 and $70,000, depending on the organization.

Work Environment

Field naturalists spend a majority of their working hours outdoors. Depending on the location, the naturalist must work in a wide variety of weather conditions. Remote sites are common, and long periods of working alone or in small teams is not uncommon for field research and management. Heavy lifting, hauling, working with machinery, digging, planting, and harvesting are all common tasks. One wildlife manager in Montana spent days literally running up and down snow-covered mountains, attempting to track down a mountain lion. Clearly, this can be a physically demanding job.

Indoor work includes scheduling, planning, and classroom teaching. Data gathering and maintaining records are also required. Naturalists may need to attend and speak at community meetings, often reading detailed legislative bills to analyze the impact of legislation before it becomes law.

Those in supervisory positions are often so busy with administrative and organizational tasks that they may spend little of their workday outdoors. Work that includes guided tours and walks through nature areas is frequently seasonal and usually dependent on daily visitors.

Full-time naturalists usually work about 35 to 40 hours per week. Overtime is usually required, and for those naturalists working in areas visited by campers, camping season is extremely busy and can require much overtime. Wildlife and range managers may be on call during storms and severe weather. Seasonal work, such as burn season for land managers and stewards, may require overtime and frequent weekend work.

Naturalists have special occupational hazards, such as working with helicopters, small airplanes, all-terrain vehicles, and other modes of transport through rugged landscapes and into remote regions. Adverse weather conditions and working in rough terrain make illness and injury more likely. Naturalists must be able to get along with the variety of people using the area and may encounter armed individuals who are poaching or otherwise violating the law.

Naturalists also have a number of unique benefits. Most prominent is the chance to live and work in some of the most beautiful places in the world. For many individuals, the lower salaries are offset by the recreational and lifestyle opportunities afforded by living and working in such scenic areas. In general, occupational stress is low, and most naturalists appreciate the opportunity to continually learn about and work to improve the environment.

Outlook

The outlook for naturalists is expected to be fair in the first decade of the 21st century. While a growing public concern about environmental issues may cause an increased demand for naturalists, this trend could be offset by government cutbacks in nature programs. Reduced government spending on education may indirectly affect the demand for naturalists, as school districts would have less money to spend on outdoor education and recreation. Despite the limited number of available positions, the number of well-qualified applicants is expected to remain high.

For More Information

For information on environmental expeditions, contact:

Earthwatch Expeditions, Inc.
PO Box 75
Maynard, MA 01754-0075
Tel: 978-461-0081
Web: http://www.earthwatch.org/

For information about internships, career conferences, and publications, such as the Environmental Career Resources Guide, *contact:*

Environmental Careers Organization
179 South Street
Boston, MA 02111
Tel: 617-426-4375
Web: http://www.eco.org/

This group offers internships and fellowships for college and graduate students with an interest in environmental issues. For information, contact:

Friends of the Earth
1025 Vermont Avenue, NW
Washington, DC 20005
Tel: 877-843-8687
Web: http://www.foe.org

For information on environmental issues, services, events, news, and job listings, check out the following Web sites:

Institute for Global Communications
18 DeBoom Street
San Francisco, CA 94107
Tel: 415-442-0220
Web: http://www.econet.org

National Wildlife Federation
11100 Wildlife Center Drive
Reston, VA 20190-5362
Tel: 800-822-9919
Web: http://www.nwf.org

Oceanographers

Biology Chemistry	School Subjects
Communication/ideas Technical/scientific	Personal Skills
Indoors and outdoors One location with some travel	Work Environment
Bachelor's degree	Minimum Education Level
$30,000 to $66,000 to $100,000+	Salary Range
None available	Certification or Licensing
About as fast as the average	Outlook

Overview

Oceanographers obtain information about the ocean through observations, surveys, and experiments. They study the physical, chemical, and biological composition of the ocean and the geological structure of the seabed. They also analyze phenomena involving the water itself, the atmosphere above it, the land beneath it, and the coastal borders. They study acoustical properties of water so that a comprehensive and unified picture of the ocean's behavior may be developed. A *limnologist* is a specialist who studies fresh water life.

History

The oceans hold some 97 percent of the water on Earth and cover more than two-thirds of its surface. Oceans hold food, chemicals, and minerals, yet oceanography is a fairly new science. In fact, according to the Oceanography Society, it was only during the 20th century that we got the first global glimpse of how the oceans work. With such inventions as deep-sea diving gear, scuba, and the bathysphere (a steel diving sphere for deep-sea observation), scientists are undertaking more detailed studies of underwater life. Oceanography includes studying air and sea interaction in weather forecasting, solving sea mining problems, predicting and preventing pollution, studying sea life, and improving methods of deriving foods from the ocean.

The Job

Oceanographers collect and study data about the motions of ocean water (waves, currents, and tides), marine life (sea plants and animals), ore and petroleum deposits (minerals and oils contained in the nodules and oozes o the ocean floor), and the contour of the ocean floor (ocean mountains, valleys, and depths). Many of their findings are compiled for maps, charts, graphs, and special reports and manuals.

Oceanographers may spend some of their time on the water each year gathering data and making observations. Additional oceanographic work is done on dry land by people who infrequently go to sea. Experiments using models or captive organisms may be conducted in the seaside laboratory.

Oceanographers use equipment designed and manufactured in special shops. This equipment includes devices to measure depths by sound impulses, special thermometers to measure water temperatures, special cameras for underwater photography, and diving gear and machines like the bathyscaphe (a submersible ship for deep-sea exploration). In addition to such commonly used equipment, many new devices have been developed for specific types of underwater work. The oceanographer of the future may be using such tools as a hydraulic miner (a dredge to extract nodules from the ocean floor), an electronic beater (a machine used to drive fish), dye curtains, fish pumps, and instrument buoys. New technologies being developed today include satellite sensors and acoustic current-measuring devices.

The oceanographer is usually part of a highly skilled team, with each member specializing in one of the four main branches of the profession. In actual work, however, there is a tremendous amount of overlap between the four branches. *Biological oceanographers* or *marine biologists* study all aspects of the ocean's plant and animal life. They are interested in how the life develops, interacts, and adapts to its environment. *Physical oceanographers* study such physical aspects of the ocean as temperature and density, waves and currents, and the relationship between the ocean and the atmosphere. *Geological oceanographers* study the topographic features and physical composition of the ocean bottom. Their work greatly contributes to our knowledge and understanding of Earth's history. *Chemical oceanographers* and *marine geochemists* investigate the chemical composition of the water and ocean floor. They may study seawater components, pollutants, and trace chemicals, which are small amounts of dissolved substances that give an area of water a certain quality.

Oceanography jobs can be found all over the United States, and not just where the water meets the shore. Although the majority of jobs are on the Pacific, Atlantic, and Gulf coasts, many other jobs are available to the marine scientist. Universities and colleges, and federal and state agencies are the largest employers of oceanographers. International organizations, private companies, consulting firms, nonprofit laboratories, and local governments also hire them. Sometimes, they are self-employed as consultants with their own businesses.

It is difficult to project what oceanographers of the future may be doing. They may be living and working on the ocean floor. The U.S. Navy Medical Research Laboratory has conducted experiments with people living under 200 feet of water.

Requirements

High School

Because a college degree is required for beginning positions in oceanography, in high school you should take four years of college preparatory courses in science and mathematics. English, writing, and computer classes are also important.

Postsecondary Training

In college, a broad program covering the basic sciences with a major in physics, chemistry, biology, or geology is desirable. In addition, you should include courses in field research or laboratory work in oceanography where available. Graduate work in oceanography is required for most positions in research and teaching. More than 100 institutions offer programs in marine studies, and more than 35 universities have graduate programs leading to a doctoral degree in oceanography.

As a college student preparing for graduate work in oceanography, you should take mathematics through differential and integral calculus and at least one year each of chemistry and physics, biology or geology, and a modern foreign language.

Other Requirements

Personal traits helpful to a career in oceanography are a strong interest in science, particularly the physical and earth sciences; an interest in situations involving activities of an abstract and creative nature (observing nature, performing experiments, creating objects); an interest in outdoor activities such as hunting, fishing, swimming, boating, or animal care; an interest in scholarly activities (reading, researching, writing); and other interests that cut across the traditional academic boundaries of biology, chemistry, and physics.

You should have above-average aptitudes in verbal, numerical, and spatial abilities. Prospective oceanographers should also be able to discriminate detail among objects in terms of their shape, size, color, or markings.

Exploring

Obviously, if you live near coastal regions, you will have an easier time becoming familiar with oceans and ocean life than if you are land-bound. However, some institutions may offer work or leisure-time experiences that will provide participants with opportunities to explore particular aspects of oceanography. Possible opportunities include work in marine or conservation fisheries or on board seagoing vessels, or field experiences in studying rocks, minerals, or aquatic life. If you live or travel near one of the oceanography research centers, such as Woods Hole Oceanographic Institution on Cape Cod, the University of Miami's Institute of Marine Science, or the Scripps Institution of Oceanography in California, you should plan to spend some time learning about their activities and studying their exhibits.

Volunteer work for students is often available with research teams, nonprofit organizations, and public centers such as aquariums. If you do not live near water, try to find summer internships, camps, or programs that involve travel to a coastal area. You can help pave your way into the field by learning all you can about the geology, atmosphere, and plant and animal life of the area where you live, regardless of whether water is present.

Employers

Approximately 50 percent of those working in oceanography and marine-related fields work for federal or state governments. Federal employers of oceanographers, ocean engineers, marine technicians, and those interested in marine policy include the Department of Defense, the Environmental Protection Agency, the U.S. Geological Survey, and the National Biological Survey, among others. State governments often employ oceanographers in environmental agencies or state-funded research projects.

Forty percent of oceanographers are employed by colleges or universities, where they teach, conduct research, write, and consult. The remaining 10 percent of oceanographers work for private industries such as oil companies and nonprofit organizations such as environmental societies. An increasing number of oceanographers are being employed each year by industrial firms, particularly those involved in oceanographic instrument and equipment manufacturing, shipbuilding, and chemistry.

Starting Out

Most college placement offices are staffed to help you find positions in business and industry after you graduate. Often positions can be found through friends, relatives, or college professors or through the college's placement office by application and interview. College and university assistantships, instructorships, and professorships are usually obtained by recommendation of your major professor or department chairperson. In addition, internships with the government or private industry during college can often lead to permanent employment after graduation. The American Institute of Biological Sciences maintains an employment service and lists both employers and job seekers.

Advancement

Starting oceanography positions usually involve working as a laboratory or research assistant, with on-the-job training in applying oceanographic principles to the problems at hand. Some beginning oceanographers with Ph.D. degrees may qualify for college teaching or research positions. Experienced personnel, particularly those with advanced graduate work or doctorates, can become supervisors or administrators. Such positions involve considerable responsibility in planning and policymaking or policy interpretation. Those who achieve top-level oceanographer positions may plan and supervise research projects involving a number of workers, or they may be in charge of an oceanographic laboratory or aquarium.

Earnings

While marine scientists are richly rewarded in nonmaterial ways for their diverse and exciting work with the sea, they almost never become wealthy by American standards. Salaries depend on education, experience, and chosen discipline. Supply and demand issues, along with where you work also come into play. Some examples of jobs in the marine sciences that presently pay more than the average include physical oceanography, marine technology and engineering, and computer modeling.

According to a 1999 report by the National Association of Colleges and Employers, those graduating with a bachelor's degree in geology and geological sciences were offered an average starting salary of $34,900. Graduates with a master's degree started at an average of $44,700.

According to the *Occupational Outlook Handbook,* in 1999, the average annual salary for experienced oceanographers working in managerial, supervisory, and nonsupervisory positions for the federal government was $66,000. Salaries for geologists, geophysicists, and oceanographers ranged from less than $30,950 to more than $101,390, with a median of $53,890.

In addition to their regular salaries, oceanographers may supplement their incomes with fees earned from consulting, lecturing, and publishing their findings. As highly trained scientists, oceanographers usually enjoy good benefits, such as health insurance and retirement plans offered by their employers.

Work Environment

Oceanographers in shore stations, laboratories, and research centers work five-day, 40-hour weeks. Occasionally, they serve a longer shift, particularly when a research experiment demands around-the-clock surveillance. Such assignments may also involve unusual working hours, depending on the nature of the research or the purpose of the trip. Trips at sea mean time away from home for periods extending from a few days to several months. Sea expeditions may be physically demanding and present an entirely different way of life: living on board a ship. Weather conditions may impose some hazards during these assignments. Choosing to engage in underwater research may mean a more adventuresome and hazardous way of life than in other occupations. It is wise to discover early whether or not life at sea appeals to you so that you may pursue appropriate jobs within the oceanography field.

Many jobs in oceanography, however, exist in laboratories, offices, and aquariums, with little time spent underwater or at sea. Many oceanographers are needed to analyze samples brought to land from sea; to plan, develop, and organize sea-faring trips from land; and to teach. Oceanographers who work in colleges or universities get the added benefit of the academic calendar, which provides time off for travel or research.

Outlook

Although the field of marine science is growing, researchers specializing in the popular field of biological oceanography, or marine biology, will face competition for available positions and research funding over the next few years. However, funding for graduate students and professional positions is expected to increase during the coming decade in the areas of global climate change, environmental research and management, fisheries science, and marine biomedical and pharmaceutical research programs. Although job availability is difficult to predict for several years out, anyone doing good strong academic work with a well-known professor in the field has good employment chances.

In the 1990s, the largest demand in oceanography and marine-related fields was for physical and chemical oceanographers and ocean engineers, says The Oceanographic Society. Demand and supply, however, are difficult to predict and can change according to the world market situation; for example, the state of the offshore oil market can affect demand for geological and geophysical oceanographers. The U.S. Department of Labor expects employment for oceanographers to grow about as fast as the average through 2008.

The march of technology will continue to create and expand job opportunities for those interested in the marine sciences. As ways of collecting and analyzing data become more advanced, many more research positions are opening up for microbiologists, geneticists, and biochemists, fields that were limited by the capabilities of past technology but now are rapidly expanding. All these fields can have ties to the marine biological sciences. In general, oceanographers who also have training in other sciences or in engineering will probably have better opportunities for employment than those with training limited to oceanography.

The Oceanographic Society says the growing interest in understanding and protecting the environment will also create new jobs. Careers related to fisheries resources, including basic research in biology and chemistry, as well as mariculture and sea ranching, will also increase. Because the oceans hold vast resources of commercially valuable minerals, employment opportunities will come from pharmaceutical and biotechnology companies and others interested in mining these substances for potential "miracle drugs" and other commercial uses. Continued deep-sea exploration made possible by under-water robotics and autonomous seacraft may also create more market opportunities for underwater research, with perhaps more international than U.S.-based employment potential.

For More Information

For information about oceanography careers, contact:

About Oceanography
Texas Sea Grant College Program
Texas A&M University
PO Box 1675
Galveston, TX 77553-1675
Web: http://www-ocean.tamu.edu/Careers/

For a 24-page color brochure entitled Careers in Oceanography and Marine-Related Fields, *contact:*

The Oceanography Society
5912 LeMay Road
Rockville, MD 20851-2326
Tel: 301-881-1101
Email: TOS.Service@tos.org
Web: http://www.tos.org/

For additional career information, contact the following organizations:

American Geophysical Union
2000 Florida Avenue, NW
Washington, DC 20009
Tel: 800-966-2481
Web: http://www.agu.org/

American Institute of Biological Sciences
1444 Eye Street, NW, Suite 200
Washington, DC 20005
Tel: 202-628-1500
Email: admin@aibs.org
Web: http://www.aibs.org/careers/

Ocean Engineering Society
Institute of Electrical and Electronics Engineers
345 East 47th Street
New York, NY 10017-2394
Web: http://ewh.ieee.org/soc/oes/oes.html

Scripps Institution of Oceanography
0-233 University of California, San Diego
9500 Gilman Drive
La Jolla, CA 92093-0233
Web: http://www.sio.ucsd.edu/

Technical Committee on Acoustical Oceanography
Acoustical Society of America
2 Huntington Quadrangle, Suite 1NO1
Melville, NY 11747-4502
Tel: 516-576-2360
Web: http://asa.aip.org/tech_com/ao.html

Pharmacologists

School Subjects
Biology
Chemistry
Mathematics

Personal Skills
Communication/ideas
Technical/scientific

Work Environment
Primarily indoors
Primarily one location

Minimum Education Level
Doctorate degree

Salary Range
$40,000 to $75,000 to $100,000+

Certification or Licensing
Voluntary

Outlook
Faster than the average

Overview

Pharmacologists play an important role in medicine and in science by studying the effects of drugs, chemicals, and other substances on humans and animals. These highly educated scientists conduct research on living tissues and organs to determine how drugs and other chemicals act at the cellular level. Their results help to discover how drugs should be most effectively used. The study of pharmacology is necessary to standardize drug dosages; analyze chemicals, food additives, poisons, insecticides, and other substances; and identify dangerous substances and harmful levels of controlled chemicals.

History

Pharmacology is not the same as pharmacy. Pharmacology is the science concerned with the interactions between chemicals and biological systems. Pharmacy is the practice of preparation and dispensing of drugs to patients.

Past civilizations, especially the cultures of ancient Greece and China, compiled the earliest written pharmacological knowledge, identifying certain diseases and the recommended "prescriptions" for these ailments. It was not until thousands of years later that organized experiments in pharmacology began. Many credit Francois Magendie, an early 19th-century French physiologist, with the birth of experimental pharmacology. The research of Magendie and his student, Claude Bernard, on poisons such as strychnine and carbon monoxide, and on the use of curare as a muscle relaxant, helped to establish many of the principles of modern pharmacology. In 1847, a German, Rudolf Bucheim, started the first institute of pharmacology at the University of Dorpat, establishing the study of pharmacology as a singular discipline. A student of Bucheim, Oswald Schmiedeberg, became a professor of pharmacology and further passed on his knowledge to students from all over the world. One of these students, John Jacob Abel, is attributed to bringing experimental pharmacology to the United States.

The medical achievements and discoveries of pharmacologists are numerous. Their work has helped in the development of antibiotics, anesthetics, vaccines, tranquilizers, vitamins, and many other substances in wide medical use today. Pharmacologists have been instrumental, for example, in the use of ether and other anesthetics that have modernized surgical procedures. Their research was used in the development of lifesaving drugs such as penicillin, tetanus and polio vaccines, antimalaria drugs, and countless other compounds. In addition, pharmacologists have helped to develop drugs to treat heart disease, cancer, and psychiatric illnesses.

With the scientific advances of the early 20th century, especially the introduction of antibacterial drugs into medicine, pharmacology gained recognition as a distinct discipline. Spurred by pharmacological research, the Food, Drug, and Cosmetic Act of 1938 was introduced, requiring rigorous studies of drugs before they could be marketed. Regulations continue today through the Food and Drug Administration.

Unlike early pharmacologists who were strictly devoted to developing new drugs, modern pharmacologists perform a much broader range of activities. They test pesticides for harmful reactions, identify poisons and their effects, analyze industrial pollutants, study food preservatives and colorings, and check other substances for their effects on the environment as well as on humans. Their research includes all aspects of modern molecular and cellular biology as well as effects of drugs in animals and humans.

The Job

Pharmacologists must train and study extensively in order to discover the chemical agents that cure, lessen, or prevent disease. They perform research in laboratories using cultured cells, laboratory animals, plants, and human tissues to study the effects of drugs, chemicals, or other substances. In recent years, the field of pharmacology has branched beyond pure medical research to toxicological research involving substances used in the environment, agriculture, and industry. Pharmacologists have become active in identifying hazardous substances, such as lead, mercury, and ammonia, in the workplace, in pesticides, in food preservatives and colorings, and even in common household items such as paints, aerosol sprays, and cleaning fluid.

Most pharmacologists specialize in a particular type of research. Those specializing in drug research study the effects of medical compounds upon specific organs or bodily systems, taking note of any potentially harmful side effects. By identifying the positive and negative effects of a drug, pharmacologists are able to predict its usefulness against specific diseases and recommend proper dosages and circumstances in which a drug should be administered.

Pharmacologists may choose to specialize in a particular part of the human body. *Neuropharmacologists* focus on drugs relating to the nervous system, including the brain, spinal cord, and nerves. *Cardiovascular pharmacologists* specialize in the effects of drugs relating to the cardiovascular and circulatory systems. *Endocrine pharmacologists* study drug effects on the hormonal balance of the body. *Molecular pharmacologists* study the biochemical interactions between drug molecules and cells.

Other types of pharmacologists include *biochemical pharmacologists,* who use biochemistry, cell biology, and physiology to determine how drugs interact and influence the chemical makeup of an organism, and *veterinary pharmacologists,* who are experts on the use and study of drugs with animals. Within the past 20 years, there has been a widespread use of psychotropic drugs, or drugs that influence mood and behavior patterns. *Behavioral pharmacologists* identify and develop these drugs for use in animals and humans.

Clinical pharmacologists specialize strictly in testing various drugs and compounds on human subjects. It is not uncommon for teams of pharmacologists to work together, especially in the development of more complex drugs and compounds capable of treating numerous diseases.

Dr. Dennis Mungall is the director of clinical pharmacology and anticoagulation services at a family practice residency. His clinical research involves cardiovascular medicine and coagulation disorders. He also works as a teacher, helping physicians-in-training, pharmacy students, and general health care providers understand drug therapies and side effects. "I teach how to streamline care," he says, "so that it's cost-effective and easy for the patients. I teach them how to pick the best therapy that fits the patient's pathology. Drug-drug interactions can cause adverse effects; I teach how to understand these and how to avoid them." Mungall says this work is a science of tailoring drug therapy to the individual patient.

In addition to the teaching and clinical responsibilities, Mungall also does a lot of multimedia work. He has developed software programs for teaching that capture clinical experience. "It is the experience of seeing patients face-to-face," he says, "but using computer technology." Mungall has also been published in many journals including *Clinical Pharmacology and Therapeutics.*

Requirements

High School

You should take science courses, such as physics, physical chemistry, biology, molecular biology, and organic and physical chemistry. You should also take advanced math courses (including calculus), computer science, and statistics. Courses in English and speech will also prove useful for future writing and presenting research reports.

Postsecondary Training

All pharmacologists must earn a Ph.D. or other doctoral degree. The Ph.D. in pharmacology is usually earned at an accredited medical or pharmacy school. Because pharmacology is so intimately related with the practice of medicine, many pharmacologists are also medical doctors (M.D.s); some pharmacologists who specialize in animal pharmacology are doctors of veterinary medicine (D.V.M.s). Many courses in pharmacology closely resemble medical school courses. The best places to study pharmacology are large university medical centers that offer degrees for a variety of medical disciplines. Certain veterinary schools offer degrees in veterinary pharmacology as well.

A professional organization of pharmacologists, the American Society for Pharmacology and Experimental Therapeutics provides a list of accredited pharmacology graduate programs as well as other relevant information. Once you've been accepted to such an institution, the Ph.D. program requires four to five years of study. This study involves intensive courses in cellular and molecular biology, physiology, neuroscience, basic and molecular pharmacology, chemotherapy, toxicology, statistics, and research. The major portion of the Ph.D. program requires students to undertake independent and supervised research and successfully complete an original laboratory project. Graduate students must also write a doctoral thesis on their research project.

After receiving their Ph.D., many pharmacologists go on to complete two to four additional years of postdoctoral research training assisting a scientist on a second project in order to gain further research skills and experience.

Certification or Licensing

Pharmacologists may choose to become certified within a special area of study. The Board of Clinical Pharmacology offers certification in clinical and applied pharmacology. Applicants are judged based on training and experience. They must first receive their doctoral degree and complete five years of postdoctoral research before being eligible for the exam.

Other Requirements

"Communication is the most important part of the job," says Dr. Dennis Mungall. "You'll be organizing patients, administrators, people in business, and others—bringing people together for projects." Mungall also emphasizes creativity. "Being creative," he says, "adds to your ability to be a good researcher, to be a good thinker."

Pharmacologists must be creative, curious, and flexible in order to entertain new ideas or investigative strategies. They need to be patient and willing to work long hours in order to master research that does not provide quick or easy answers. They must also be able to work alone or with similarly dedicated and driven colleagues to the conclusion of a project.

Exploring

The best way to learn about pharmacology is to interview professionals in the career. Your high school counselor or science teacher may be able to arrange an interview with a qualified pharmacologist or even help plan a tour of a pharmacological facility.

Medical and other laboratories frequently employ part-time personnel to assist with various tasks. Information regarding summer or part-time opportunities can be obtained by contacting work-study or student research programs and student placement services. But you need to keep in mind that these positions can be hard to come by because you may be competing with pharmacological graduate students for jobs.

The American Society for Pharmacology and Experimental Therapeutics provides information on the field of pharmacology, including educational programs and academic institutions, the various subspecialties of pharmacology, and laboratories, drug companies, and other branches of the profession that employ pharmacologists. Some of these subspecialties have organizations and professional societies, such as the American Society of Pharmacognosy (the study of natural drugs), the American College of Neuropsychopharmacology (the study of drugs on the nervous system), the American Society of Veterinary Physiologists and Pharmacologists, and the American Academy of Clinical Toxicology.

Employers

Pharmacologists are employed as faculty in medical, dental, veterinary, or pharmacy schools, or as researchers in large hospitals, medical centers, or research institutes. They also work for government research foundations such as the National Institutes of Health, the Environmental Protection Agency, and the Food and Drug Administration.

Starting Out

Drug companies, research organizations, medical, dental, and pharmacy schools and universities, and federal and state governments often recruit pharmacologists while they are in the process of earning their doctorates. By the second year of their doctoral program, most pharmacologists have chosen a subspecialty and seek out employers representing their chosen area.

Graduates interested in pharmacology should consult their school's placement office for job leads or send out resumes directly to research institutes or pharmaceutical and chemical companies. Pharmacological journals also provide a list of employment opportunities.

Advancement

Most beginning pharmacologists start out in academics at the assistant professor level or work in laboratories, assisting advanced pharmacologists in research. Beginning pharmacologists work to improve their laboratory procedures, learn how to work with the Food and Drug Administration and various other government agencies, and gain experience testing drugs and other substances on both animal and human subjects. In research institutes, private industry, and academic laboratories, advancement in the field of pharmacology usually means moving into a supervising position, overseeing other scientists in a laboratory setting and heading up major research projects. Pharmacologists who work as teachers advance by serving as department heads, supervising research laboratories at universities, presenting public papers, and speaking at major conferences.

Pharmacologists often view their advancements in terms of successful research projects. Dr. Dennis Mungall is looking forward to branching out into other areas to combine his interests in pharmacology, writing, and the Internet. "I have a grant from the American Heart Association to do just that," he says, "using the Internet to improve health care communication with patients."

Earnings

A 1997 survey (the most recent information available) by the American Association of Pharmaceutical Scientists places average salaries for pharmacologists at $84,500 a year for those working in industry, $78,600 for those in academia, and $74,200 for those in government. Normally, higher-salaried pharmacologists are those who supervise teams of people in larger laboratory or university settings, or are senior faculty in academic departments of pharmacology. Other benefits include health and dental insurance and paid vacation and sick days.

Work Environment

Pharmacologists work in academic settings or laboratories and generally work 40 hours a week, though they may sometimes be required to work extra hours to monitor experiments that need special attention. Most laboratories associated with academic or major research institutions are clean, well-lit, pleasant workplaces equipped with the sophisticated instruments necessary for modern research. Because pharmacologists perform such a vital role with respect to drug and chemical research, their laboratories tend to be fairly up-to-date.

Pharmacologists often work on projects that require months of effort and show seemingly slow progress; the average Food and Drug Administration approval time for new drugs is 10 years. Pharmacologists must be able to deal with the potential stress associated with working in close quarters with other professionals.

In some cases, pharmacologists are called upon to work with forensic biologists, coroners, or others involved in determining causes of death under specific circumstances. They may also be asked to travel to other research institutions to share their findings.

Outlook

Health care and related industries in general are expected to continue to expand; as a result, employment opportunities in drug companies, hospitals, medical and pharmacy schools, and government agencies involved in pharmacological research will continue to be strong.

Teaching opportunities should be plentiful as schools, universities, and medical centers will need qualified pharmacologists to train future students.

The growing elderly population will require pharmacologists to conduct more drug research and development. Pharmacology is also crucial in the development of drugs to battle existing diseases and medical conditions such as AIDS, muscular dystrophy, and cancer, and to facilitate the success of organ transplants.

Further study into drug addiction, gene therapy, and the effect of chemical substances on the environment, including their relationship to cancer and birth defects, will provide research opportunities for qualified pharmacologists. The increasing interest in more nontraditional medical treatments will also open doors to pharmacologists in such subspecialties as herbal pharmacology, which focuses on the medicinal values of plants.

In general, pharmacologists with the most advanced and updated education will have the best prospects in future expanding and specialized job markets.

For More Information

For information on student chapters, fellowship opportunities, and pharmacology careers, contact the following associations:

American Association of Pharmaceutical Scientists
2107 Wilson Boulevard, Suite 700
Arlington, VA 22201-3046
Tel: 703-243-2800
Email: aaps@aaps.org
Web: http://www.aaps.org

American Society for Pharmacology and Experimental Therapeutics
9650 Rockville Pike
Bethesda, MD 20814-3995
Tel: 301-530-7060
Email: info@aspet.org
Web: http://www.faseb.org/aspet

For information on certification, contact:

Board of Clinical Pharmacology
PO Box 40278
San Antonio, TX 78229-1278
Tel: 210-567-8505
Web: http://www.abcp.net

Toxicologists

Biology Chemistry Mathematics	School Subjects
Helping/teaching Technical/scientific	Personal Skills
Primarily indoors Primarily one location	Work Environment
Bachelor's degree	Minimum Education Level
$30,000 to $50,000 to $200,000	Salary Range
Recommended	Certification or Licensing
About as fast as the average	Outlook

Overview

Toxicologists design and conduct studies to determine the potential toxicity of substances to humans, plants, and animals. They provide information on the hazards of these substances to the federal government, private businesses, and the public. Toxicologists may suggest alternatives to using products that contain dangerous amounts of toxins, often by testifying at official hearings. There are approximately 9,000 toxicologists currently employed in the United States.

History

The study of the effects of poisons (toxins) began in the 1500s when doctors documented changes in body tissues of people who died after a long illness. Although research was hampered by the lack of sophisticated research equipment, physicians and scientists continued to collect information on the causes and effects of various diseases over the next 300 years.

As microscopes and other forms of scientific equipment improved, scientists were able to study in greater detail the impacts of chemicals on the human body and the causes of disease. In the mid-1800s, Rudolf Virchow, a German scientist, considered to be the founder of pathology (the study of diseased body tissue) began to unlock the mystery of many diseases by studying tissues at the cellular level. His research of diseased cells helped pathologists pinpoint the paths diseases take in the body.

With society's increasing dependence on chemicals (for example, in agriculture, industry, and medicine) and growing use of prescribed (and illegal) drugs, the study of the impact of these potential toxins on public health and environmental quality has become more important. The toxicologist's role in determining the extent of a problem, as well as suggesting possible alternatives or antidotes, plays an important role in society. They act as consultants on developing long-term solutions to problems such as air and water pollution, the dumping of toxic waste into landfills, and the recognition of an unusual reaction to a pharmaceutical drug.

The Job

As scientists, toxicologists are concerned with the detection and effects of toxins, as well as developing methods to treat intoxication (poisonings). A primary objective of a toxicologist is to protect consumers by reducing the risks of accidental exposure to poisons. Toxicologists investigate the many areas in which our society uses potential toxins and documents their impact. For example, a toxicologist may chemically analyze a fish in a local lake to read for mercury, a harmful toxin to humans if consumed in high enough levels. This reading is reported to government or industry officials, who, in turn, write up a legal policy setting the maximum level of mercury that manufacturing companies can release without contaminating nearby fish and endangering consumers.

On many projects, a toxicologist may be part of a research team, such as at a poison control center or a research laboratory. *Clinical toxicologists* may work to help save emergency drug overdose victims. *Industrial toxicologists* and *academic toxicologists* work on solving long-term issues, such as studying the toxic effects of cigarettes. They may focus on research and development, working to improve and speed up testing methods without sacrificing safety. Toxicologists use the most modern equipment, such as electron microscopes, atomic absorption spectrometers, and mass spectrometers, and study new research instrumentation that may help with sophisticated research.

Industrial toxicologists work for private companies, testing new products for potential poisons. For example, before a new cosmetic good can be sold, it must be tested according to strict guidelines. Toxicologists oversee this testing, which is often done on laboratory animals. These toxicologists may apply the test article ingredients topically, orally, or by injection. They test the results through observation, blood analysis, and dissection and detailed pathologic examination. Research results are used for labeling and packaging instructions to ensure that customers use the product safely. Although animal experimentation has created a great deal of controversy with animal-rights supporters, humane procedures are stressed throughout toxicology studies.

Toxicologists carefully document their research procedures so that they can be used in later reports on their findings. They often interact with lawyers and legislators on writing legislation. They may also appear at official hearings designed to discuss and implement new policy decisions.

Because toxic materials are often handled during research and experimentation, a toxicologist must pay careful attention to safety procedures.

Requirements

High School

While in high school, you can best prepare for a career as a toxicologist by taking courses in both the physical and biological sciences (chemistry and biology, for example), algebra and geometry, and physics. English and other courses that improve written and verbal communications skills will also be useful since toxicologists must write and report on complicated study results.

Postsecondary Training

Most toxicologists obtain their undergraduate degrees in a scientific field, such as pharmacology or chemistry. Course work should include mathematics (including mathematical modeling), biology, chemistry, statistics, biochemistry, pathology, anatomy, and research methods.

Career opportunities for graduates with bachelor's degrees are limited; the majority of toxicologists go on to obtain master's or doctorate degrees. Graduate programs vary depending on field of study, but may include courses such as pathology, environmental toxicology, and molecular biology. Doctorate programs generally last four to five years.

Certification or Licensing

Certification recognizes an individual's competence and expertise in toxicology and can enhance career opportunities. The American Board of Toxicologists certifies toxicologists after they pass a comprehensive two-day examination and complete the necessary educational requirements. To be eligible, applicants with a bachelor's degree in an appropriate field must first have 10 years of work experience; with a master's degree, seven years; and with a doctorate degree, three years.

Other Requirements

Toxicologists must be hard workers and be dedicated to their field of study. To succeed in their work, they must be careful observers and have an eye for detail. Patience is also necessary, since many research projects can last months to years and show little results. The ability to work both alone and as part of a team is also needed for research.

Because of the nature of their work, toxicologists must also realize the potential dangers of working with hazardous materials. They must also be comfortable working with laboratory animals and be able to dissect them to examine organs and tissues. Though efforts have been made to limit and control live animal experimentation, research still requires their use to identify toxins and, in turn, protect the consumer public.

Exploring

If you are interested in pursuing a career as a toxicologist, consider joining a science club in addition to taking biology and chemistry courses to further develop your laboratory skills. Your career counselor might be able to help you arrange a discussion with a practicing toxicologist to explore career options. Part-time jobs in research laboratories or hospitals are an excellent way to explore science first-hand, although opportunities may be limited and require higher levels of education and experience.

Employers

According to the Society of Toxicology, approximately 9,000 toxicologists are employed in the United States. A recent job market survey of Ph.D.s shows that 47 percent work for chemical and pharmaceutical companies, 21 percent are employed by large universities or medical schools, and 14 percent work in government. An increasing number (12 percent) work for consulting firms, providing professional recommendations to agencies, industries, and attorneys about issues involving toxic chemicals. Nonprofit research foundations employ only 4 percent of all toxicologists.

Starting Out

Those with the necessary education and experience should contact the appropriate research departments in hospitals, colleges and universities, government agencies, or private businesses. Often, school professors and career placement advisors provide job leads and recommendations.

Networking with professionals is another useful way to enter the field. Past work with a team of toxicologists during graduate study may open doors to future research opportunities. Membership in a professional society can also offer more networking contacts. In addition, the Society of Toxicology and the American College of Medical Toxicology both offer job placement assistance to members.

Advancement

Skilled toxicologists will find many advancement opportunities, although specific promotions depend on the size and type of organization where the toxicologist is employed. Those working for private companies may become heads of research departments. Because of their involvement in developing important company policy, highly skilled and respected toxicologists may become vice presidents or presidents of companies. Obviously, this type of promotion would entail a change in job responsibilities, involving more administrative tasks than research activities.

Toxicologists working for educational institutions may become professors, heads of a department, or deans. Toxicologists who want to continue to research and teach can advance to positions with higher pay and increased job responsibilities. Toxicologists working at universities usually write grant proposals, teach courses, and train graduate students. University positions often do not pay as well as industrial positions, but they offer more independence in pursuing research interests.

Earnings

As trained professionals, toxicologists have good earning potential. Wages vary depending on levels of experience, education, and employer. According to a 1998 salary survey by the Society of Toxicology, toxicologists with a bachelor's degree earned an average of $30,000 a year; with a master's degree, $50,000; and those with a Ph.D., $160,000 or more. Toxicologists with 20 or more years of experience can earn up to $200,000 per year, particularly if they work in the consumer product or pharmaceutical industries. Toxicologists working for the government usually make less than those working in industry.

Salaries for toxicologists are, in general, on the rise, but the survey reports that the biggest factor determining earning potential is not location, but type of employer. Certification also plays a large role in salary level; toxicologists who are certified earn higher salaries than those who have not earned certification. Comparing gender differences, the salary survey found that women continue to be paid less than their male counterparts.

Work Environment

Toxicologists usually work in laboratories or offices, in teams or alone. Research in libraries or in the field is a major part of the job. Some toxicologists work a standard 40-hour workweek, although many work longer hours. Overtime should be expected if an important research project is on deadline. Research and experimentation can be both physically and mentally tiring, with much of the laboratory work and analysis done while under time restrictions. Some travel may be required to testify at hearings, collect field samples, or to attend professional conferences.

Toxicologists often work on research that has important health considerations. At a poison control center, for example, toxicologists may try to find information about the poisonous properties of a product while an overdose victim's life is in danger. Because their work involves studying the impact of toxic material, toxicologists must be willing to handle contaminated material and adhere to strict safety precautions.

Outlook

Employment opportunities for toxicologists are expected to continue to be good. The growing use of chemicals and pharmaceuticals by society has created demand for trained professionals to determine and limit the health risks associated with potential toxins. However, according to the Society of Toxicology, the job market for toxicologists, especially in traditional fields, is expected to be tight. Job opportunities should be greatest in large urban areas where many large hospitals, chemical manufacturers, and university research facilities are located. Those with the most training and experience will have the best prospects in finding employment.

For More Information

For certification information, contact:

American Board of Toxicology
PO Box 30054
Raleigh, NC 27622-0054
Tel: 919-847-8720
Web: http://www.abtox.org

For additional information, contact the following organizations:

American College of Medical Toxicology
777 East Park Drive
PO Box 8820
Harrisburg, PA 17105-8820
Web: http://www.acmt.net

Society of Toxicology
1767 Business Center Drive, Suite 302
Reston, VA 20190
Tel: 703-438-3115
Web: http://www.toxicology.org

Veterinary Technicians

Biology Chemistry	School Subjects
Helping/teaching Technical/scientific	Personal Skills
Primarily indoors Primarily one location	Work Environment
Associate's degree	Minimum Education Level
$15,000 to $20,161 to $59,000	Salary Range
Required by certain states	Certification or Licensing
About as fast as the average	Outlook

Overview

Veterinary technicians provide support and assistance to veterinary doctors. They work in a variety of environments, including zoos, animal hospitals, clinics, private practices, kennels, and laboratories. Work may involve large or small animals, or both. Although most veterinary technicians work with domestic animals, some professional settings may require treating exotic or endangered species. There are approximately 32,000 veterinary technicians employed in the United States.

History

As the scope of veterinary practices grew and developed, veterinarians began to require assistants. At first the role was informal, with assistants being trained by the veterinarians they worked for. In the latter half of the 20th century, however, the education, and thus the profession, of veterinary assistants became formalized.

The Job

Many pet owners depend upon veterinarians to maintain the health and well-being of their pets. Veterinary clinics and private practices are the primary settings for animal care. In assisting veterinarians, veterinary technicians play an integral role in the care of animals within this particular environment.

A veterinary technician is the person who performs much of the laboratory testing procedures commonly associated with veterinary care. In fact, approximately 50 percent of a veterinary technician's duties involves laboratory testing. Laboratory assignments usually include taking and developing X rays, performing parasitology tests, and examining various samples taken from the animal's body, such as blood and stool. A veterinary technician may also assist the veterinarian with necropsies in an effort to determine the cause of an animal's death.

In a clinic or private practice, a veterinary technician assists the veterinarian with surgical procedures. This generally entails preparing the animal for surgery by shaving the incision area and applying a topical antibacterial agent. Surgical anesthesia is administered and controlled by the veterinary technician. Throughout the surgical process, the technician tracks the surgical instruments and monitors the animal's vital signs. If an animal is very ill and has no chance for survival or an overcrowded animal shelter is unable to find a home for a donated or stray animal, the veterinary technician may be required to assist in euthanizing it.

During routine examinations and checkups, veterinary technicians will help restrain the animals. They may perform ear cleaning and nail clipping procedures as part of regular animal care. Outside the examination and surgery rooms, veterinary technicians perform additional duties. In most settings, they record, replenish, and maintain pharmaceutical equipment and other supplies.

Veterinary technicians also may work in a zoo. Here, job duties, such as laboratory testing, are quite similar, but practices are more specialized. Unlike in private practice, the zoo veterinary technician is not required to explain treatment to pet owners; however, he or she may have to discuss an animal's treatment or progress with zoo veterinarians, zoo curators, and other zoo professionals. A zoo veterinary technician's work also may differ from private practice in that it may be necessary for the technician to observe the animal in its habitat, which could require working outdoors. Additionally, zoo veterinary technicians usually work with exotic or endangered species. This is a very competitive and highly desired area of practice in the veterinary technician field. Currently there are only 50 zoo veterinary technicians working in the United States. There are only a few zoos in each state; thus, a limited number of job opportunities exist within these zoos. To break into this area of practice, veterinary technicians must be among the best in the field.

Another setting where veterinary technicians work is research. Most research opportunities for veterinary technicians are in academic environments with veterinary medicine or medical science programs. Again, laboratory testing may account for many of the duties; however, the veterinary technicians participate in very important animal research projects from start to finish.

Technicians are also needed in rural areas. Farmers require veterinary services for the care of farm animals such as pigs, cows, horses, dogs, cats, sheep, mules, and chickens. It is often essential for the veterinarian and technician to drive to the farmer's residence because animals are usually treated on site.

Another area in which veterinary technicians work is that of animal training, such as at an obedience school or with show business animals being trained for the circus or movies. Veterinary technicians may also be employed in information systems technology, where information on animals is compiled and provided to the public via the Internet.

No matter what the setting, a veterinary technician must be an effective communicator and proficient in basic computer applications. In clinical or private practice, it is usually the veterinary technician who conveys and explains treatment and subsequent animal care to the animal's owner. In research and laboratory work, the veterinary technician must record and discuss results among colleagues. In most practical veterinary settings, the veterinary technician must record various information on a computer.

Requirements

High School

A high school diploma is necessary in order to obtain the required training. High school students who excel at math and science have a strong foundation on which to build. Those who have had pets or who simply love animals and would like to work with them also fit the profile of a veterinary technician.

Postsecondary Training

The main requirement is the completion of a two- to four-year college-based accredited program. Upon graduation, the student receives an associate's or bachelor's degree. Currently, there are over 75 accredited programs in the United States. A few states do their own accrediting, using the American Veterinary Medical Association and associated programs as benchmarks.

Most accredited programs offer thorough course work and preparatory learning opportunities to the aspiring veterinary technician. Typical courses include mathematics, chemistry, humanities, biological science, communications, microbiology, liberal arts, ethics/jurisprudence, and basic computers.

Once the students complete this framework, they move on to more specialized courses. Students take advanced classes in animal nutrition, animal care and management, species/breed identification, veterinary anatomy/physiology, medical terminology, radiography and other clinical procedure courses, animal husbandry, parasitology, laboratory animal care, and large/small animal nursing.

Veterinary technicians must be prepared to assist in surgical procedures. In consideration of this, accredited programs offer surgical nursing courses. In these courses, a student learns to identify and use surgical instruments, administer anesthesia, and monitor animals during and after surgery.

In addition to classroom study, accredited programs offer practical courses. Hands-on education and training are commonly achieved through a clinical practicum, or internship, where the student has the opportunity to work in a clinical veterinary setting. During this period, a student is continuously evaluated by the participating veterinarian and encouraged to apply the knowledge and skills learned.

Certification or Licensing

Although the American Veterinary Medical Association determines the majority of the national codes for veterinary technicians, state codes and laws vary. Most states offer registration or certification, and the majority of these states require graduation from an accredited program as a prerequisite for taking the examination. Most colleges and universities assist graduates with registration and certification arrangements. To keep abreast of new technology and applications in the field, practicing veterinary technicians may be required to complete a determined amount of annual continuing education courses.

Exploring

High school students can acquire exposure to the veterinary field by working with animals in related settings. For example, a high school student may be able to work as a part-time animal attendant or receptionist in a private veterinary practice. Paid or volunteer positions may be available at kennels, animal shelters, and training schools. However, direct work with animals in a zoo is unlikely for high school students.

Employers

Veterinary technicians are employed by veterinary clinics and animal hospitals, zoos, schools and universities, and animal training programs. In rural areas, farmers hire veterinary technicians as well as veterinarians. Jobs for veterinary technicians in zoos are relatively few, since there are only a certain number of zoos across the country. Those veterinary technicians with an interest in research should seek positions at schools with academic programs for medical science or veterinary medicine. The majority of veterinary technicians find employment in animal hospitals or private veterinary practices, which exist all over the country. However, there are more job opportunities for veterinary technicians in more densely populated areas.

Starting Out

Veterinary technicians who complete an accredited program and become certified or registered by the state in which they plan to practice are often able to receive assistance in finding a job through their college's placement offices. Students who have completed internships may receive job offers from the place where they interned.

Veterinary technician graduates may also learn of clinic openings through classified ads in newspapers. Opportunities in zoos and research facilities are usually listed in specific industry periodicals such as *Veterinary Technician Magazine* and *AZVT News*, a newsletter published by the Association of Zoo Veterinary Technicians.

Advancement

Where a career as a veterinary technician leads is entirely up to the individual. Opportunities are unlimited. With continued education, veterinary technicians can move into allied fields such as veterinary medicine, nursing, medical technology, radiology, and pharmacology. By completing two more years of college and receiving a bachelor's degree, a veterinary technician can become a veterinary technologist. Advanced degrees can open the doors to a variety of specialized fields. There are currently efforts to standardize requirements for veterinary technicians. A national standard would broaden the scope of educational programs and may create more opportunities in instruction for veterinary professionals with advanced degrees.

Earnings

Earnings are generally low for veterinary technicians in private practices and clinics, but pay scales are steadily climbing due to the increasing demand. Better-paying jobs are in zoos and in research. Those fields of practice are very competitive, especially zoos, and only a small percentage of highly qualified veterinary technicians are employed in them.

About 70 percent of veterinary technicians are employed in private or clinical practice and research. According to the American Veterinary Medical Association, graduates of accredited veterinary technology programs with work experience earned between $15,000 and $59,000 a year in a high-end industry job in 1999. The average yearly salary of veterinary technicians is $20,161. Earnings vary depending on practice setting, geographic location, level of education, and years of experience. Benefits vary and depend on each employer's policies.

Work Environment

Veterinary technicians generally work 40-hour weeks, which may include longer weekdays and Saturdays. Their hours also fluctuate during emergencies.

Veterinary technicians must be prepared for the unexpected. In field or farm work, they may have to face rough weather while treating animals. Injured animals can be very dangerous, and veterinary technicians have to exercise caution when caring for them. Technicians also handle animals that are diseased or infested with parasites. Some of these conditions, such as ringworm, are contagious, so the technician must take precautions to prevent the spread of diseases.

People who become veterinary technicians care about animals. In private practice, technicians get to know the animals and are able to track progress. In other areas, such as zoo work, veterinary technicians work with very interesting, sometimes endangered, species. This work can be challenging and rewarding in the sense that they are helping to save a species and continuing efforts to educate people about these animals. Veterinary technicians who work in research gain satisfaction from knowing their work contributes to promoting both animal and human health.

Outlook

Employment for veterinary technicians will grow about as fast as the average for all other occupations through 2008, according to the U.S. Department of Labor. Veterinary medicine is a field that is not adversely affected by the economy, so it does offer stability. The public's love for pets coupled with higher disposable incomes will encourage continued demand for workers.

For More Information

For more information on careers, contact the following organizations:

American Veterinary Medical Association
1931 North Meacham Road, Suite 100
Schaumburg, IL 60173
Tel: 847-925-8070
Web: http://www.avma.org

Association of Zoo Veterinary Technicians
4401 Zoo Parkway
Asheboro, NC 27203
Tel: 336-879-7636
Web: http://www.worldzoo.org/azvt

North American Veterinary Technician Association
PO Box 224
Battle Ground, IN 47920
Web: http://www.avma.org/navta/

Zoologists

	School Subjects
Biology Chemistry English	
	Personal Skills
Communication/ideas Technical/scientific	
	Work Environment
Indoors and outdoors Primarily one location	
	Minimum Education Level
Bachelor's degree	
	Salary Range
$27,930 to $46,140 to $86,020+	
	Certification or Licensing
None available	
	Outlook
About as fast as the average	

Overview

Zoologists are biologists who study animals. They often select a particular type of animal to study, and they may study an entire animal, one part or aspect of an animal, or a whole animal society. There are many areas of specialization from which a zoologist can choose, such as origins, genetics, characteristics, classifications, behaviors, life processes, and distribution of animals.

History

Human beings have always studied animals. Knowledge of animal behavior was a necessity to prehistoric humans, whose survival depended on their success in hunting. Those early people who hunted to live learned to respect and even revere their prey. The earliest known paintings, located in the Lascaux Caves in France, depict animals, which demonstrates the importance of animals to early humans. Most experts believe that the artists who painted those images viewed the animals they hunted not just as a food source, but also as an important element of spiritual or religious life.

The first important developments in zoology occurred in Greece, where Alcmaeon, a philosopher and physician, studied animals and performed the first known dissections of humans in the sixth century BC. Aristotle, however, is generally considered to be the first real zoologist. Aristotle, who studied with the great philosopher Plato and tutored the world-conquering Alexander the Great, had the lofty goal of setting down in writing everything that was known in his time. In an attempt to extend that knowledge, he observed and dissected sea creatures. He also devised a system of classifying animals that included 500 species, a system that influenced scientists for many centuries after his death. Some scholars believe that Alexander sent various exotic animals to his old tutor from the lands he conquered, giving Aristotle unparalleled access to the animals of the ancient world.

With the exception of important work in physiology done by the Roman physician Galen, the study of zoology progressed little after Aristotle until the middle of the 16th century. Between 1555 and 1700, much significant work was done in the classification of species and in physiology, especially regarding the circulation of blood, which affected studies of both animals and humans. The invention of the microscope in approximately 1590 led to the discovery and study of cells. In the 18th century, Swedish botanist Carl Linnaeus developed the system of classification of plants and animals that is still used.

Zoology continued to develop at a rapid rate, and in 1859, Charles Darwin published *On the Origin of Species,* which promoted the theory of natural selection, revolutionized the way scientists viewed all living creatures, and gave rise to the field of ethology, the study of animal behavior. Since that time, innumerable advances have been made by zoologists throughout the world.

In the past century, the rapid development of technology has changed zoology and all sciences by giving scientists the tools to explore areas that had previously been closed to them. Computers, submersibles, spacecraft, and tremendously powerful microscopes are only a few of the means that modern zoologists have used to bring new knowledge to light. In spite of these advances, however, mysteries remain, questions go unanswered, and species wait to be discovered.

The Job

Although zoology is a single specialty within the field of biology, it is a vast specialty that includes many major subspecialties. Some zoologists study a single animal or a category of animals, whereas others may specialize in a particular part of an animal's anatomy or study a process that takes place in many kinds of animals. A zoologist might study single-cell organisms, a particular variety of fish, or the behavior of groups of animals such as elephants or bees.

Many zoologists are classified according to the animals they study. For example, *entomologists* are experts on insects, *ichthyologists* study fish, *herpetologists* specialize in the study of reptiles and amphibians, *mammalogists* focus on mammals, and *ornithologists* study birds. *Embryologists,* however, are classified according to the process that they study. They examine the ways in which animal embryos form and develop from conception to birth.

Within each primary area of specialization there is a wide range of subspecialties. An ichthyologist, for example, might focus on the physiology, or physical structure and functioning, of a particular fish; on a biochemical phenomenon such as bioluminescence in deep-sea species; on the discovery and classification of fish; on variations within a single species in different parts of the world; or on the ways in which one type of fish interacts with other species in a specific environment. Others may specialize in the effects of pollution on fish or in finding ways to grow fish effectively in controlled environments in order to increase the supply of healthy food available for human consumption.

Some zoologists are primarily teachers, while others spend most of their time performing original research. Teaching jobs in universities and other facilities are probably the most secure positions available, but zoologists who wish to do extensive research may find such positions restrictive. Even zoologists whose primary function is research, however, often need to do some teaching in the course of their work, and almost everyone in the field has to deal with the public at one time or another. As Dr. R. Grant Gilmore, a fish ecologist who is a senior scientist and former director of marine science at the Harbor Branch Oceanographic Institute, says, "In marine science, it's a public day, too. You do get reporters calling about odd things all the time. That happens. People don't realize that, but you end up going before the public eye whether you want to or not."

Students often believe that zoological scientists spend most of their time in the field, observing animals and collecting specimens. In fact, most researchers spend no more than two to eight weeks in the field each year. Zoologists spend much of their time at a computer or on the telephone. Speaking of his daily activities, Gilmore says, "Getting up and starting with correspondence is, I think, number one. We communicate with colleagues all the time, and with the young people wanting to get into the field, and that's one thing we try to get out right away. We try to get letters and telephone calls returned. That's another thing. I think most people think they're going to be out in the boat, diving. No. You communicate. You communicate with the granting agencies, people that are going to support you. You communicate with the people that are going to work for you, or students. There's an awful lot of that going on. Part of my day, two or three hours, is devoted to that, and that alone. And then it's a joy to get to your data."

It is often the case that junior scientists spend more time in the field than do senior scientists, who study specimens and data collected in the field by their younger colleagues. Senior scientists spend much of their time coordinating research, directing younger scientists and technicians, and writing grant proposals or soliciting funds in other ways.

Raising money is an extremely important activity for zoologists who are not employed by government agencies or major universities. The process of obtaining money for research can be time-consuming and difficult. Gilmore, an expert fund-raiser, views it as the most difficult part of his job. Good development skills can also give scientists a flexibility that government-funded scientists do not have. Government money is sometimes available only for research in narrowly defined areas that may not be those that a scientist wishes to study. A zoologist who wants to study a particular area may seek his or her own funding in order not to be limited by government restrictions.

Requirements

High School

A high school student who wants to prepare for a career in zoology should begin by making certain that he or she gets a well-rounded high school education. Although a solid grounding in biology and chemistry is an absolute necessity, the student should remember that facility in English will also be invaluable. Writing monographs and articles, communicating with colleagues both orally and in writing, and writing persuasive fund-raising proposals are all activities at which scientists need to excel. The student should also read widely, not merely relying on books on science or other subjects that are required by the school. The scientist-in-training should search the library for magazines and journals dealing with areas that are of personal interest. Developing the habit of reading will help prepare students for the days when they must keep up with the latest developments in the field while doing research and performing various other tasks. Computer skills are also essential, since most zoologists not only use the computer for writing, communication, and research, but also use various software packages to perform statistical analyses.

Postsecondary Training

Dr. Gilmore recommends that college students who are interested in zoology avoid specializing at the undergraduate level: "I would say the best bet is to get a really good liberal arts degree and emphasize the sciences. If you're interested in biology, emphasize the biological sciences. And then, your graduate level is when you really make up your mind which direction you're going to go. But if you have the aptitude for the sciences, I think you should try a number of the different sciences. Just play the field when you can." Too many students specialize too soon and discover later that the field they have chosen is not the one for which they are best suited.

A bachelor's degree is essential for a zoologist, and advanced degrees are highly recommended, but no licensing or other certification is required, and there is no zoologists' union. Academic training, practical experience, and the ability to work effectively with others are the most important prerequisites for a career in zoology.

Other Requirements

Success in zoology requires tremendous effort. It would be unwise for a person who wants to work an eight-hour day to become a zoologist, since hard work and long hours (sometimes 60 to 80 hours per week) are the norm. Also, although some top scientists are paid extremely well, the field does not provide a rapid route to riches. A successful zoologist finds satisfaction in work, not in a paycheck. The personal rewards, however, can be tremendous. The typical zoologist finds his or her work satisfying on many levels.

A successful zoologist is generally patient and flexible. A person who cannot juggle various tasks will have a difficult time in a job that requires doing research, writing articles, dealing with the public, teaching students, soliciting funds, and keeping up with the latest publications in the field. Flexibility also comes into play when funding for a particular area of study ends or is unavailable. A zoologist whose range of expertise is too narrowly focused will be at a disadvantage when there are no opportunities in that particular area. A flexible approach and a willingness to explore various areas can be crucial in such situations, and a too-rigid attitude may lead a zoologist to avoid studies that he or she would have found rewarding.

An aptitude for reading and writing is a must for any zoologist. A person who hates to read would have difficulty keeping up with the literature in the field, and a person who cannot write or dislikes writing would be unable to write effective articles and books. Publishing is an important part of zoological work, especially for those who are conducting research.

Exploring

One of the best ways to find out if you are suited for a career as a zoologist is to talk to zoologists and find out exactly what they do. Contact experts in your field of interest. If you are interested in birds, find out whether there is an ornithologist in your area. If there is not, find an expert in some other part of the country. Read books, magazines, and journals to find out who the experts are. Don't be afraid to write or call people and ask them questions.

One good way to meet experts is to attend meetings of professional organizations. If you are interested in fish, locate organizations of ichthyologists by searching in the library or on the Internet. If you can, attend an organization's meeting and introduce yourself to the attendees. Ask questions and learn as much as you can.

Try to become an intern or a volunteer at an organization that is involved in an area that you find interesting. Most organizations have internships, and if you look with determination for an internship, you are likely to find one.

Employers

Zoologists are employed by a wide variety of institutions, not just zoos. Many zoologists are teachers at universities and other facilities, where they may teach during the year while spending their summers doing research. A large number of zoologists are researchers; they may be working for nonprofit organizations (requiring grants to fund their work), scientific institutions, or the government. Of course, there are many zoologists who are employed by zoos, aquariums, and museums. While jobs for zoologists exist all over the country, large cities that have universities, zoos, museums, and so forth will provide far more opportunities for zoologists than will rural areas.

Starting Out

Before you get your first job as a zoologist, you will need to have at least a bachelor's degree. For the best results, you will need a master's degree. It is possible to find work with a bachelor's degree, but it is likely that you will need to continue your education to advance in the field. Competition for jobs among those who have doctoral degrees is fierce, and it is often easier to break into the field with a master's than it is with a Ph.D. For this reason, many people go to work after they receive a master's degree and get a doctorate while they are working.

According to Dr. R. Grant Gilmore, the best way to get your first job in zoology is "to make contacts. Make as many personal contacts as possible. And try to get a qualified scientist to help you out with that; someone who really knows the field and knows other people. If your adviser doesn't, try to find one who does. It's so competitive right now that the personal contact really makes a difference."

You will be ahead of the game if you have made contacts as an intern or as a member of a professional organization. It is an excellent idea to attend the meetings of professional organizations, which generally welcome students. At those meetings, introduce yourself to the scientists you admire and ask for their help and advice. Gilmore says, "I see too many students these days hesitating to go up to that renowned scientist and talk to him. Just go up and carry on a conversation. They seem to be afraid to do that. I think that's a big mistake."

Don't be shy, but be sure to treat people with respect. Ultimately, it's the way you relate to other people that determines how your career will develop. Says Gilmore, "I don't care what GPA you have. I don't care what SAT score you have or GRE score you have. That does not make one bit of difference. Everybody has high scores these days. It's the way you present yourself, your interests, the way you act. And that personal contact that makes all the difference."

Advancement

Higher education and publishing are two of the most important means of advancing in the field of zoology. The holder of a Ph.D. will make more money and have a higher status than the holder of a bachelor's or master's degree. The publication of articles and books is important for both research scientists and professors of zoology. A young professor who does not publish cannot expect to become a full professor with tenure, and a research scientist who does not publish the results of his or her research will not become known as an authority in the field. In addition, the publication of a significant work lets everyone in the field know that the author has worked hard and accomplished something worthwhile.

Because zoology is not a career in which people typically move from job to job, people generally move up within an organization. A professor may become a full professor; a research scientist may become known as an expert in the field or may become the head of a department, division, or institution; a zoologist employed by an aquarium or a zoo may become an administrator or head curator. In some cases, however, scientists may not want what appears to be a more prestigious position. A zoologist who loves to conduct and coordinate research, for example, may not want to become an administrator who is responsible for budgeting, hiring and firing, and other tasks that have nothing to do with research.

Earnings

A study conducted by the National Association of Colleges and Employers determined that beginning salaries in private industry in 1999 averaged $29,000 for holders of bachelor's degrees in biological science (including zoologists), $34,450 for those with master's degrees, and $45,700 for holders of doctoral degrees.

According to the *Occupational Outlook Handbook,* the median annual wage for biological scientists in 1998 was $46,140, with the middle 50 percent earning between $35,200 and $67,850. The bottom 10 percent earned less than $27,930, while the top 10 percent made more than $86,020. In 1997, general biological scientists employed by the federal government earned an average salary of $48,600.

It is possible for the best and brightest of zoologists to make substantial amounts of money. Occasionally, a newly minted Ph.D. who has a top reputation may be offered a position that pays $80,000 or more per year, but only a few people begin their careers at such a high level.

The benefits that zoologists receive as part of their employment vary widely. Employees of the federal government or top universities tend to have extensive benefit packages, but the benefits offered by private industry cover a wide range, from extremely generous to almost nonexistent.

Work Environment

There is much variation in the conditions under which zoologists work. Professors of zoology may teach exclusively during the school year or may both teach and conduct research. Many professors whose school year consists of teaching spend their summers doing research. Research scientists spend some time in the field, but most of their work is done in the laboratory. There are zoologists who spend most of their time in the field, but they are the exceptions to the rule.

Zoologists who do fieldwork may have to deal with difficult conditions. A gorilla expert may have to spend her time in the forests of Rwanda; a shark expert may need to observe his subjects from a shark cage. For most people in the field, however, that aspect of the work is particularly interesting and satisfying.

Zoologists spend much of their time corresponding with others in their field, studying the latest literature, reviewing articles written by their peers, and making and returning phone calls. They also log many hours working with computers, using computer modeling, performing statistical analyses, recording the results of their research, or writing articles and grant proposals.

No zoologist works in a vacuum. Even those who spend much time in the field have to keep up with developments within their specialty. In most cases, zoologists deal with many different kinds of people, including students, mentors, the public, colleagues, representatives of granting agencies, private or corporate donors, reporters, and science writers. For this reason, the most successful members of the profession tend to develop good communication skills.

Outlook

According to the *Occupational Outlook Handbook,* the significant job growth that the field of zoology (and other fields of biology) experienced from the 1980s to the middle 1990s has slowed. There are still jobs available, but competition for good positions—especially research positions—is increasing. Much of the decrease in growth has been caused by government budget cuts. It is expected, however, that growth will increase in the early 21st century, spurred partly by the need to analyze and offset the effects of pollution on the environment.

Those who are most successful in the field in the future are likely to be those who are able to diversify. Dr. Gilmore, who believes that the need for well-trained zoologists will increase in the next century, advises those entering the field to stay open-minded, maintain a wide range of contacts, and keep an eye out for what is occurring in related fields: "This is a danger in science today. People become so narrowly focused that it endangers their future. There's an ecological concept which I like to use that says 'Diversity is stability.' If you put all your marbles in one basket and somebody tips that basket, you're done for. Keep an open mind and keep open contacts."

For More Information

For information on careers, schools, internships and job opportunities, check out the following Web sites or contact:

American Association of Zoo Keepers
3601 29th Street, SW, Suite 133
Topeka, KS 66614
Web: http://www.aazk.org/

American Institute of Biological Sciences
1444 I Street, NW, Suite 200
Washington, DC 20005
Tel: 202-628-1500
Web: http://www.aibs.org

American Zoo and Aquarium Association
8403 Colesville Road, Suite 710
Silver Spring, MD 20910-3314
Tel: 301-562-0777
Web: http://www.aza.org

The following society publishes the bimonthly journal, American Zoologist, *and is probably the best single source of information about all areas and aspects of zoology. For more information, contact:*

Society for Integrative and Comparative Biology
1313 Dolley Madison Boulevard, Suite 402
McLean, VA 22101
Tel: 800-955-1236
Web: http://www.sicb.org

Index